O Blest Communion!

O Blest Communion!

THE HOME LIFE OF THE
CHURCH OF ENGLAND

Betty Saunders

DARTON · LONGMAN + TODD

First published in 1996 by
Darton, Longman and Todd Ltd
1 Spencer Court
140–142 Wandsworth High Street
London SW18 4JJ

ISBN 0–232–52144–1

A catalogue record for this book is available from the British Library

Phototypeset in 10/13.5pt New Century Schoolbook by Intype London Ltd
Printed and bound by Page Bros, Norwich

CONTENTS

CHURCH OF ENGLAND PEOPLE have a particular vocation, which is to be at home. Home is where the heart is, and most of the action, too. The C of E lives among the neighbours, in the parochial system and the familiar church buildings everyone likes to see on the skyline, and that is the message which comes out strongly, time and time again, as one talks with the people in the parishes, women and men, clergy and laity. This is a tribute to them as they tell their own stories.

They are the ones on the ground who carry the burdens joyfully, who really want to worship the Lord in the beauty of holiness on behalf of those who are not present, who will somehow find the money to keep the Church of England in business for its most important function: being there.

The Revd Gillean Craig, Rector of St George's-in-the-East, on the fringes of London's docklands, makes a case for the seemingly eccentric view that the C of E should stop pretending to be a missionary Church. 'Missionaries are sent out from one place to proclaim their faith in another,' he wrote in the *Church Times* (2 February 1996) under the headline 'Nowhere to go – but somewhere to be'.

'Just think about it: what sort of missionaries already own the oldest, most beautiful and most expensive building in the neighbourhood? The truth is, of course, that this place *is* our home,' he wrote. 'The community that makes up our parish is ours, and we belong to it. We're not sent out to be somewhere different: we're baptised to *be* different, but (nearly all of us) to stay where we are.'

The stories from the parishes show that staying home is not a quiet life, even if you disregard the scandals that make the news, and the doings of the mavericks, which attract most of the publicity. Signs of growth belie the popular belief that falling numbers spell out the Church's doom.

There are changes in the air which reach all the way from the highest level of Church government in Westminster to every parochial church council sitting with its tea and biscuits. After they had absorbed the shock of an £800 million reduction in the Church Commissioners' assets, people began to realise that life could never be the same again; but they saw, also, that they were presented with a challenge that could be like a shot in the arm: an end to complacency, and a sorting out of priorities.

The Church of England is being streamlined at the centre, its structures radically altered, its policy-making machinery reviewed. Some members of the General Synod were concerned about proceeding with too much speed, but when such matters were debated in February 1996, a Sheffield member, Professor David McClean, did not think the pace of change would worry most people in the parishes; and however he meant it, he was not far wrong.

Some church people are politically conscious, well-tuned-in to happenings at the top, and perhaps more should be; but most parishioners hardly ever think about the General Synod and its agenda. Their own agenda seems more immediate. This is acknowledged in the report of the Archbishops' Commission on the Organisation of the Church of England, *Working As One Body*, which is the source of the changes to come. It says: 'The parish church is the main focus of the spiritual lives of most Anglicans. Its energy and vitality, or its lassitude and ineffectiveness, impinge most closely upon the way people are nurtured in faith.' So it is, and so it will be.

CHAPTER ONE

Strangers and Pilgrims

While we debate and agonise about how to reach the unchurched millions, they are flocking into our churches in unprecedented numbers.... (Jeremy Martineau, the Church of England National Rural Officer, in Country Way*)*

'IT'S ALL IN THE STONES,' says the Revd Michael Tingle, the Vicar of Burford, in Oxfordshire, making it sound like a clue from a treasure-hunt, which it is. The treasure is whatever people are looking for when they push open the church door and take the first tentative steps into the silence within: silence because this is a weekday and not a Sunday, when the scenery and the characters will be different. Sundays are another story.

Twenty-two people in a thousand will be in Church of England churches on Sunday, a total of about 1,090,400 out of a population of 40 million: a few more than will be going to football on Saturday, but a small enough score to make the Church bewail what it says is the secularisation of society, the cheerful indifference of a populace which seems to be immune to the best attempts at evangelisation. Yet it may be that the Sunday morning car-washers are not the only ones who are deaf to good news, for there really are sermons in stones. These are the sermons which deliver the kind of message picked up by the missing millions.

There were 35 million visits made to parish churches alone in 1993, without counting the cathedrals, and the evidence is that the number of those who come looking for something – no one is quite sure what – is growing all the time. While the Church scans the horizon for the sheep it cannot find, the flocks are drifting into the sheep-pens, from where they will promptly drift out again, because people who go visiting churches are not about to turn into church-goers. But they are the raw material of mission, and the gift they bring with them is a huge opportunity for the expansion of the Church's ministry.

People need icons, and the parishes know that. The presence of the tourists vindicates the few who carry the burden of the buildings, who will always raise the money for the roof, the spire, the rewiring, the restoration of fabric eroded by time and weather. Parishes would vote with the Council for the Care of Churches, which says the church buildings are tools of mission. 'If the Church's main concern is to give witness to the Gospel in the world, could there be a more effective tool than the buildings the Church possesses in every village, city and town in the country?' the council says in a report called *Mission in Mortar: the role of the church building in the Decade of Evangelism.*

'At the centre of Christianity is the Incarnation, the mystery whereby God took earthly form and made visible the immaterial in this material world. So surely the Church need not be ashamed of having prominent physical symbols of its faith in buildings erected for God's glory, and known as places whither Christians come to worship and whence they go out to serve in God's name . . .' the council continues. 'So providing a ministry to the visitor should be regarded not as a sop to the tourist industry but as an obvious way to promote evangelism.' The report quotes from T. S. Eliot's poem 'The Rock': 'When the stranger says: "What is the meaning of this city?" . . . What will you answer?'

Part of the answer might not need words at all. The unceasing round of the Church's liturgy, and the prayers prayed over the centuries, are stored in the walls, and some, at least, of those who filter through will be made aware that there is more to be discovered in a church than interesting memorials. 'It's all in the stones.'

The challenge, as the Church's rural officers see it, is to turn visitors into pilgrims. 'The notion of pilgrimage is the most vibrant theological concept in present-day culture,' according to Canon Andrew Bowden, of Gloucester, quoted in *Country Way.* 'Why have you come today?' was one of the questions put to visitors when Southwell Minster held a survey a few years ago. Of the 2946 out of 4575 who filled in the form, 765 had lit a candle, and 520 used the Pilgrim's Chapel for prayer or a few quiet moments. They came, in many cases, for 'Something I need'.

Michael Tingle, who was speaking after ten years at Burford, is one of many clergy and lay people who are working on the need to provide a few spiritual pointers for people who may not want them, or do not know that they do. Burford Parish Church is in the big league, with 100,000 visitors a year. 'Some come because they are interested in architecture or history. We have a number of experts passing through. They even come to study the lichens outside.

'We've an aisle called the Bartholomew Aisle, and a lot come from the States because they think they have links with the Bartholomew family. But whoever they are, when they visit they are open to picking up things like the free leaflets we put out: *To Help you pray, What is this life?* and *The Two Great Commandments*. Thousands of leaflets are taken in a year. We're always putting them out, and we see people leave with all three. It's something they wouldn't get elsewhere. We don't put them near the cards that are on sale, but in a side chapel, on a table tomb, and they're available at all the five churches in the group.

'There was a young girl who picked one up about two years ago, and on her way back to Ireland she died on the ferry, from gas inhalation. The leaflet was found in her luggage, and used at her funeral, and it came back to us. They wanted us to know.

'If people are looking for something, we try to provide it, which is something all churches can do, and it's a great opportunity, because the churches are in a very privileged position. Our buildings speak of stability. We keep all five churches open in the daytime, and it's not an expensive operation. We've no verger, it's done by volunteers, on a shoestring. We keep our costs to a minimum.'

Most churches cannot be open all the time, but they can all be open sometimes. Inspiration came to Sandy Marchant, a laywoman in Worcestershire, when she leafed through the list of gardens which open on specified days under the National Gardens Scheme. 'I said to my friend, "Wouldn't that be a good idea for churches?" ' The result is the Through the Church Door project, based in the The Hay Loft of the Old Vicarage at Stoulton, in Worcestershire, which has mobilised a network of country churches in Herefordshire, Worcestershire, south Shropshire, south-west Warwickshire and parts of Gloucestershire. They all describe themselves in a gazetteer which lists happenings where visitors can join parishioners, from Rogationtide walks to flower festivals and pig roasts.

Sandy Marchant used to help with the visitors at Lichfield Cathedral, and while she was there the cathedral sponsored her for a heritage management course. She says: 'I focused all my training on the Church, particularly on country churches, so I started with some country churches on Romney Marshes. The Countryside Commission publishes leaflets about local walks, and they always say "Stop at the churches", but with so many locked doors and outdated notices I worried about the message people would get if they did stop. Through the Church Door began when I moved from Lichfield to Worcestershire.'

She has a Non-Conformist background, which is useful, she says. 'It helps when I try to anticipate what visitors might be interested in, because if you grow up in a tradition you take things for granted, but when you change in middle life, you look at it a different way. One difficulty I had at Lichfield was taking people to the shrine of St Chad. I remember a canon saying that medieval pilgrims would come to venerate the skull of Chad, and I found that very hard. I couldn't cope with what seemed like idolatry, and I wondered what message the children would take away. It made me think how I would answer, and that challenge is the challenge of Through the Church Door. How do you make sense of evidence you see in a church building? I want people to think about it.'

There is a series of training sessions behind her project. 'Where do you place yourself physically in relation to your visitors? In a cathedral it's easy, you can let people be in charge of their own visit, but not in tiny churches. How do you enable those who want to be on their own to be so without feeling neglected? What about those who are burning with questions? People don't always want to be spoken to as soon as they come in. Well, I don't always want to talk. It's very much a question of trying to anticipate being on the receiving end, of trying to read body language.'

Mrs Marchant says: 'A soft, subtle approach is right for English people. I shall never forget a canon of Lichfield who always saw the beauty of things, and for me it was being shown the fluted edge of a gothic pillar, the touch of a hand on the stone. It changed the course of all I have done.'

What do they know of the Church of England, who only buildings know? The volunteer welcomers soon find out how little knowledge there is, and learn to give gentle answers back again, as Mrs Alexander's defunct hymn for children advises. 'Oh, yes, we still hold services here, the notices are in the porch. Yes, monks and nuns still exist, and in our Church, too, certainly. Well, we pay for the upkeep, actually; those of us who come here on Sundays. We have to keep the place afloat so that it's there when people need it, because that's what the Church of England is for. It's for everyone.'

Many who come will not know what their own vicar looks like, unless they have been to the church fête and thrown wet sponges at him. 'Lady vicars' are simply part of the scenery to those who have no interest in parties and divisions within parties, or in the two integrities the Church is trying to maintain in order to hold itself together after the ordination of women to the priesthood. Even the consequences of the £800 million shrinkage of the Church Commissioners' assets are not very visible to non-church-goers, though they have changed the life of every diocese and parish in England.

Open the church door and the smells are the same as ever: Brasso, polish, and must, flowers fresh or unfresh, damp rising, and occasionally, a whiff of incense. But for those who are middle-aged or older it is not the same Church into which they were baptised or ordained.

The *Alternative Service Book 1980* ousted the 1662 *Book of*

Common Prayer, even though the Prayer Book is still officially the book of Church. There will be a revised *ASB* in the year 2000, and by then a whole stack of little extras as new liturgies continue to roll off the presses. Feelings still run high. In a church down in Devon, a visitor threw the new book back at a churchwarden, so the Revd Bill Blakey reports (in his Grove Ethical Studies No. 82). 'He then boomed out his preferred version of the service whilst we were using the one in the book. No one complained, because it was known that he put a £20 note in the collection.'

It would be hard to know where to start looking for the vicar in most English villages today. The Sheffield scheme, devised in the 1970s, swept the clergy out of the countryside and into places with big populations and a good deal less historic loyalty to the Church. Lay people must take on many of the duties now; but while all the talk is of the part the laity can play, the role of the priest is not defined, and there is confusion and loss of spirit among many clergy. The requirement for clergy assessments along the lines of those applied to sales representatives is threatening. Often it only adds to a growing sense of insecurity.

Across the Malvern Hills, on the Worcestershire-Herefordshire border, where there are five priests for the twenty-two parishes in the Ledbury deanery, the Rural Dean, the Revd Carl Attwood, thinks the clergy must learn to let go, but he says, 'Going about wearing a long black cassock and a dog collar is quite distinctive. People always look for a focus in the community, and the part about being the focus is the good thing.' He himself is a focus easy to spot, even though he does not sport a long black cassock in his own two parishes.

'Carl is a colourful character in more ways than one. He wears brilliant colours and all sorts of odd garments, and he has the quickest brain I've ever met,' says the deanery lay chairman, Brian Beves, who has been a member of the General Synod of the Church of England. 'He's a fine musician; he could have made a career of it. Jazz, too; and counselling. He does it all on top of everything else. At the end of a social evening, at one in the morning, he'll say, "I must do some work." And he'll go and visit someone who's dying. The life he leads makes me go pale.'

Being a focus still matters; but Carl Attwood says, 'Just as important is the fact that the Church is made up of everybody, that the Church is touching people's lives: not the old knee-jerk reaction of "We haven't been visited by the Church because the Rector hasn't been." In the country everyone expects the Church to know when you're ill, you belong to the fabric of the community; but five clergy can't do that over twenty-two parishes.'

He has been frustrated, he says, by one or two Trollopian characters, yet he feels for them. 'It's wrong if you totally devalue the role of the parish priest, but it's up to the clergy to be able to let go. I filled in my assessment form. "What are your faults? What do others think are your faults?" We had a staff meeting the next day, and I said, "Just tell me what you think, and I'll fax it to the Bishop." The weak points they mentioned were uncannily accurate, and I didn't like it. My wife said to me several days later, "You're still smarting." Now I'm a very open sort of chap and if *I* sting, then it's very hard for clergy built on the old model.'

There is always the thought that most things go round in a circle. In *Francis Kilvert and His World*, Frederick Grice, of the Kilvert Society, quotes the Methodist historian, E. Jones, whose glum picture of the scene on the Welsh border in 1721 rings a faint bell today, for what is now known as 'the Sunday gallop' was in full swing then as hard-up curates sped from church to church to earn their ten or twelve pounds a year. 'These churches were many miles distant, so that the Sunday round was a kind of perpetual motion for the curate, hurrying from place to place like a hasty itinerant, with little opportunity for refreshment or rest. The times of the services depended largely on his ability to manage his rounds.' So what is new? Yet by Kilvert's time, in the mid-nineteenth century, things were looking up and the Church was embarking on a period of renaissance – perhaps as now.

In Kilvert's last parish of Bredwardine, where he lies buried in the churchyard, the present Rector, the Revd Paul Byllam-Barnes is sanguine about his five churches. 'We do have cars now, and there were three services a Sunday in each church in those days. Now there is one in each, which wouldn't be possible without help from lay people: the churchwardens and two lay Readers. We have one locally ordained priest who does two services a month. I do four services a Sunday, mostly holy communions, and three churches have evensong as their main service of the day. It's a real liturgical cocktail, with the *Book of Common Prayer* predominating. We get 120 to 130 in the five churches every Sunday out of a total population of 1100 including children, and if you think, "Oh, goodness, the Church of England is in decline", come and see ten per cent of the village in church.

'In terms of population it's much better than the average. We have a hefty quota [the sum set for each parish to pay to the diocese] of £18,000 a year collectively, and five church buildings to care for, but one tremendous advantage in the country is that church and community still overlap quite considerably. The church is seen as the community building, and people are tremendously interested in what happens with the building. They'll always help with fundraising.'

He found a living link with Kilvert when he moved to Kilvert's parish from the diocese of Guildford. 'Remember little Davie, the shepherd boy he buried one Christmas Day (which gives an interesting idea of the way they kept Christmas)? When we came, there was an old lady one hundred years old who was little Davie's cousin. We get a lot of visitors, but not to services, and if the visitors' book and the offertory box are anything to go by, Bredwardine, with Kilvert's grave, is the most favoured. It's a great place to be, largely because of the community, and the fact that people are prepared to be involved, though one always longs for more, especially where the worship of the church is concerned. But at parish level there are signs of hope. The parish. Yes. I'll drink to that.'

Paul Byllam-Barnes is married to Jackie, who works in an art gallery at the house across the border in Clyro, where Kilvert lived during his happiest years. She is a bell-ringer, and rings at Bredwardine, among other places. 'It's lovely here,' she says. 'It's the rainbow's end. Isn't it nice to know someone's happy in the Church of England, when there's so much misery and gloom?'

The Church of England touches life at many levels, an advantage which is neatly illustrated by the Warden of Wadham College, Oxford, John Flemming, writing in *The Wadham College Gazette* about the departure of the college chaplain, the Revd Michael Roden. 'He was able to come back for a Dorothy dinner with the Fellows [Dorothy was the sister of the college's founder] and a Rave for Rwanda with the staff (and students) before a more formal handover in the chapel. The chaplain's role in a multi-faith and little-faith community is not an easy one. Michael played a crucial role in college as counsellor and confidant of all, while adding the powerful example, which inspired an active social conscience in many of our students, to his pastoral role and ambulatory leadership. The staff party last Christmas really sprang to life when Michael went to microphone and showed us what it takes to lead a pop group.'

Michael Roden, who was succeeded at Wadham by a woman priest, the Revd Rebecca Watts, went to be Rector of Steeple Aston with North Aston and Tackley, between Oxford and Banbury. Looking back to his time at Wadham, he says: 'This set of eighteen-year-olds coming through knows very little about the Church. It's not so much that they're faithless, the attitude is, "I know I should be against what you stand for, but by the way, what is it?" It's an easier generation to deal with than mine was, because that was highly prejudiced, and this is not. It's a good opportunity for the Church, because in a sense we're starting from scratch.'

His rock and roll band soon broke the ice in his new parishes with a concert at Tackley. 'I started the group nineteen years ago, when I was sixteen, and saw no reason to stop it. It's based on long-standing friendships. You might say our secret is we haven't been spoiled by success.'

Michael's rural parishes are mixed communities now. 'When I look at them I feel it wasn't Oxford that prepared me for this, but the borough of Lambeth, where I was a curate. There are the same sort of problems; just the scenery is different. I've been amazed at how quickly people get to know things in villages, but one has to take this and learn to enjoy it.

'Our three parishes, with a population of 2000, have a quota target of £20,000, but I feel it's important to look beyond finance, though in three churches one is constantly doing repairs, and it's like running up an escalator the wrong way. In one church I suggested some new stained glass, and I was surprised how enthusiastic people were about doing something new rather than just maintaining the old; about being more adventurous. It's nice to think the Church didn't just stop in Victorian times.

'The Church of England has hung on, in cities and in the country-side, and the time has come to enjoy it a bit. It's something to celebrate that we're still here. In our Lent group someone who is not a Christian said, "I don't find any saints in the Church." I feel he hadn't looked very closely, because they are there; they're hidden characters, really, and their story needs to be told.

'A number of my generation are coming back now with their children, looking for something deeper, and they'll come to church slightly sporadically, but they're very well-intentioned, and that can be harnessed. We had a do-it-ourselves day at the church, and thirty came. It was a wonderful Saturday. Next day in church, when I wanted to thank them, they weren't there. The church thing had changed to doing something for the church on Saturday.

'Things on the ground are a lot more encouraging than in the media; in fact people take almost no notice of what's reported in the press,' Michael concluded. 'They know the Church is a flawed body, but they're interested in the hope that underlies the Church. They are post-cynical. And anyway, a lot of media people go to church and find the home that they needed there.'

There is the same sort of story in other places. At St Mary's, Twickenham, in London ['liberal Catholic, not polarised'], the Sunday School has gone from nil into three figures as an influx of young families has changed the scenario. The Vicar, the Revd Alun Glyn-Jones, says, 'The vast majority of our confirmation candidates are adults, and they stay. Gone are the days when you had forty sixteen-year-olds dressed in white and never saw them again. We've had eighty adults confirmed over the last seven years.

'We've made them and their children's noises welcome. We've created a service for new people, actually removed our 9.30 communion, and there were a fair number of brickbats, but we thought it through. It's forty-five minutes, and not threatening; it's instead of getting them to a parish communion and saying, "You can join in, but not in this bit." Then they graduate to the parish communion. We avoid the word "family" like the plague, because a third of our congregation lives on its own, and great emphasis on children puts the singles at arm's length, so they come to the new service, too. It's an adult message illustrated by children. Where we lack is in the parents of the fifteen-to-sixteen-year-olds. There are not nearly so many as in the nought-to-tens, and whether something happened about twenty years ago and we failed to pick it up . . . There used to be a time when you could visit thirty-year-olds and assume some sort of church background, but not now. They know nothing at all, and you have to start at square one, which is very interesting from our point of view.'

Keith Robinson, the Secretary of the London Stock Exchange, who is on the London Diocesan Synod, is an active member of the congregation at St Mary's – one of the singles – and he sees the arrival of the young families as a fascinating challenge. 'It's converting – though maybe that's too strong a word – changing a kind of transient, almost superficial interest in the Christian faith into something deeper, and that is difficult to do against a background of rearing young children. When we arrange mid-week events it's always the same old few who turn up. The new blood are all bathing babies, and that sort of thing.' The Stock Exchange, he says, would see it in the context of 'evolving markets'.

Mr Glyn-Jones says, 'We started an organisation for young families, but it's been a struggle. A lot of chaps – and girls, too – don't get home till eight at night, but a third of the PCC is made up of this group. A number of parishes are going the other way, and there are some highly responsive churches surrounded by those which, if we are not careful, will go to the wall. I was head of a

London comprehensive, and I know schools are the same. If the head is working like a Trojan the school will succeed in any area; and it's great fun. I'm back in parish life with all the enthusiasm of a young curate after being away from it for twenty-two years.

'Don't go over the top about us, we weep our hearts out at the failures, the people we never treated right, but we're struggling on. Now people come into a service and look round and say, "Well! We thought the churches were empty." '

CHAPTER TWO

Business as Usual

> *I suddenly tumbled to the fact that I was absolutely angry inside ... It wasn't until I realised that I really hated the Church in some ways that humour came back and depression went away. (The former Bishop of Durham, Dr David Jenkins, in an interview with* Third Way *magazine)*

WE WERE PICKING OUR WAY past the winos on the steps of his church, then on through a jungle of cement mixers and holes in the road to lunch in the canteen of the workplace where the vicar is chaplain. Charles, which is not his real name, presides over a parish not far south of the River Thames in the inner-city borough of Lambeth. 'It just needs a few more people to go over to Rome,' he says pleasantly. 'I don't see any problem about women priests. As for those who do, well, it's something in the genes, isn't it? When feelings run high, I can only explain it in terms of genes. To be charitable, I ought to respect them, but I can't see any future for those who can't accept women.'

He is a cheerful, friendly man, ruddy-faced and approachable, and he was speaking for the majority, writing off about a third of the C of E without any apparent malice, for that is the way things are. Anger is often under the surface. 'Why deny the ministry of someone else?' he says. 'The idea of being a separate church within a church is anathema, it's anti-Christian, it denigrates the body of Christ; so they'll have to go. They can go to Rome, though it's beginning to collapse about their ears. I think the Church of England is the only church which has anything going for it today.'

Charles has come back to the smoke after a longish sojourn in the outer suburbs, very leafy, rather plush, or so it seemed in a casual encounter with his previous parish. That was where we first met, when he returned there for a ruby wedding party: a marquee in the garden, flowers on the tables, and a lot of amiable Rotarians talking about golf. 'Darling Charles,' said his former women parishioners, embracing him. The Church of England can always throw up some startling contrasts.

Ironically, before he went to leafydom he had a parish across the river in London, which is now firmly in the fold of Forward in Faith, the 4000–strong umbrella organisation for priests and people opposed to women priests. His successor there wants a parallel church in the pattern which to Charles, who has a woman priest as his curate, is anathema. Charles says, 'They once asked me back for an anniversary, which was nice, but they wouldn't invite me now. My hands are contaminated.'

'Contaminated' is not a word Forward in Faith ever uses. It talks about 'impairment of communion', and spells out the meaning of that in its guidelines on relations with clergy. 'Is a female priest on the staff of the parish or group of parishes where the priest works? Does he concelebrate with women? Is he happy to act as alternate to women celebrants? Does he attend the Holy Thursday rites in the cathedral and renew his priestly vows alongside women? Where the answer to any of these, or similar questions, is yes, the impairment of communion with the diocesan bishop and his representatives might properly be thought to extend to that priest.'

The chairman of Forward in Faith, John Broadhurst, now Bishop of Fulham, has reassured opposers who fear that the code of practice might make them look at each other in a judgemental way. 'I believe they misunderstand the intention. The question for each of us has to be, "On what principles can I continue to exist as an Anglican finding myself in a new situation where I reject the orders of some of those canonically ordained?" ' He has acknowledged: 'We accept that we may prove mistaken. It is doubt about the validity of the orders conferred, and not certainty as to their invalidity, which requires us to distance ourselves from them.'

The first of about 1300 new women priests were ordained in Bristol Cathedral on 12 March 1994, a bleak day of chilling winds which whipped through the long, happy queues of parishioners waiting red-nosed by every entrance. The Forward in Faith demonstration they expected did not materialise, which was not surprising, since none was planned, but the Roman Catholic Women's Network was there with banners flapping – 'Our Turn Next'; and MOW (the Movement for the Ordination of Women), still proclaiming 'Women's Place is in the House – of Bishops'. A mile away, at Pip'n'Jay (St Philip and St Jacob's Church), the Evangelical Canon Malcolm Widdecombe, brother of the Roman Catholic convert Ann Widdecombe MP, tolled his funeral bell. He had been at her mass in the House of Commons chapel on the day of her reception, saying, 'I'm not going. I intend to stay and be a nuisance.'

There was a cheer when the Bishop of Bristol, the Rt Revd Barry Rogerson, an MOW consultant bishop, emerged looking dapper in a light grey suit and told the nearest queue, 'I don't want to hear any Anglican muttering,' meaning that what he did want to hear was a full-throated roar of affirmation when he put the question, 'Is it therefore your will that they should be ordained?' When the moment arrived the answer came in a great shout, 'It is', and a passing of the peace resembling a game of general post lasted for twenty minutes. Bristol is a very 'pro' diocese, and joy overflowed that day from the parishes which had come to see their women deacons priested. It would have seemed churlish to ask them what they thought they were doing, for the Church of England on the ground has a touching sort of innocence tied up with jumble sales and home-made marmalade, rows about the flower-rota, and the burden of beloved buildings – the affectionate, accepting C of E, which used to be home to all her sons and daughters. And anyway, nice people from the parishes can turn very mean.

A few weeks afterwards the London ordinations in St Paul's Cathedral had a harder edge. The then Bishop of London, Dr David Hope, processed in, disappeared into the sanctuary, and was seen no more. The Rev Paul Williamson, Priest-in-Charge of St George's, Hanworth, who has tried persistently to challenge the General Synod's decision on women priests in the High Court, was allowed three minutes to state his case, but angry yells from the clergy of the Willesden Area cut him off. The Bishop of Willesden, the Rt Revd Graham Dow, was the only London bishop who ordained women to the priesthood. Someone spat at Fr Williamson as he left the cathedral, but he said, 'I didn't see who.'

According to Bishop David Jenkins, the problems are only at their beginning. At the time of his retirement from Durham in July 1994 he told Roy McCloughry, an associate editor of the Bible-based *Third Way*: 'I don't know that I've said this publicly yet but I suppose it'll have to come out: I think there is a sense in which the traditionalists are quite right in being scared stiff by the ordination of women to the priesthood, which in the Catholic tradition is really the centre of authority: it must be equally shared in all respects by male and female. That clearly does challenge the whole way in which traditional Christian authority has been applied, dogmas have been worked out, the Church has been run – and of course, it does reflect back into our understanding of God.'

Before he retired in August 1995, the former Archbishop of York, Dr John Habgood – who has always been in favour of the ordination of women – told the *Church Times* that the Anglican Church had gone about it too quickly. 'My belief is that if the bishops had been allowed to set their own pace we might have avoided some of the traumas. As it was, we were pushed by the rest of the Church.' He said the most disastrous mistake was not made by the Church of England, but by the Anglican Consultative Council, who, with a very narrow majority, allowed the Episcopal Church in the USA to go ahead and ordain women – a move which pushed the rest of the Anglican Communion into an intolerable position. 'We were forced to choose between breaking up the Communion or damaging our ecumenical relations with Rome and Orthodoxy. And that I think should never have happened.'

In England, the real division comes in the fractured relationship between opposers of women's ordination and diocesan bishops who ordain women priests. It does not help if the diocesan leaves it to suffragans or assistant bishops to act on his behalf, because 'their actions are accounted his', says Forward in Faith, and 'to be unable to receive a sacrament at the hands of one whom the bishop has authorised for the purpose is to be unable to receive it from his own hands'.

In the view of the Bishop of Basingstoke, Dr Geoffrey Rowell, this goes too far, and he attracted a lot of indignation, but also a certain amount of gratitude, when he said so at a national rally of Forward in Faith in September 1994. Dr Rowell, an Oxford theologian who was Fellow, tutor and chaplain of Keble College, delivered a warning against looking for a 'pure' Church. Afterwards, in a letter to the *Church Times*, he explained his concern:

'. . . Communion is first and foremost not something which we create but which we receive. It is a gift from above. We do well to ponder the depth of meaning in the common expression "to receive communion". When we recognise this it follows that the vertical dimension of communion takes precedence over the horizontal; indeed it creates the horizontal. From this perspective, whilst Catholic Anglicans may be unable to receive communion from those whose orders have not the assurance given by Catholic consent and clear grounding in scripture and tradition, where such doubt does not obtain, as in the case of a bishop who ordains women to the priesthood, we ought not to refuse the gift, the communion, that is offered. The sacraments are, after all, Christ's sacraments.'

Unity within the Church of England now relies on the pledge by the House of Bishops to recognise and maintain 'two integrities': the two equally legitimate positions of those who accept the ministry of women priests and those who do not. The recognition is part of a process entered upon 'while the whole Church seeks to come to a common mind', says the *Bonds of Peace* document issued by the Bishops from their Manchester meeting in June 1993. 'The Church of England needs to understand itself as a communion in dialogue, committed to remaining together in the ongoing process of the discernment of truth within the wider fellowship of the Christian Church. Giving space to each other, and remaining in the highest possible degree of communion in spite of differences are crucial, as we strive to be open to the insights of the wider Christian community.'

Behind closed doors the bishops opposed to women priests fought their corner long and hard, but the unanimity of the House of Bishops held fast and not one diocesan bishop claimed his right under clause 2 of the Priests (Ordination of Women) Measure to turn his diocese into a no-go area by excluding women priests from within its boundaries.

From April 1993 through to July, the Ecclesiastical Committee in Parliament and representatives of the General Synod battled through the Measure, and in the end, although it sometimes looked as if the decision would go the other way, the committee of peers and MPs voted by 16–11 that it was 'expedient'.

Some members, notably Frank Field MP, who supported the Measure, were uneasy over the lack of any protection enshrined in law for those unable to accept the ministry of women priests. Protection is in the Act of Synod, which was subsequently passed and implemented. But that is not legally binding, only morally binding; and at some time in the future it could be withdrawn.

A Financial Provisions Measure (which sets out arrangements to compensate clergy leaving the Church over the issue of women priests) was declared expedient by 17 votes to 10. If, as Forward in Faith has forecast, 1000 priests do eventually leave, the rough estimate given to the Ecclesiastical Committee (at 1993 prices) was a net cost to the Church of £23,840,000 over twenty years, plus £36 million in net housing capital funded by the Church Commissioners over the same period. The £800 million reduction in the Church Commissioners assets was just beginning to be realised at the time, and it was apparent to the parliamentarians that the bill would be handed down to the people in the parishes.

'It is the man in the pew who will have to pay for this Measure,' said Lord Robertson of Oakridge. But so he would anyway, whatever the state of the Commissioners' finances, replied Philip Mawer, the Secretary-General of the General Synod, because the Commissioners did not have 'pots of money', and 'in no way could the person in the pew have been at any time insulated from the effects of the Measure, however well the Commissioners were doing'.

'So the person in the pew will pay for the woman in the pulpit and the man on the dole then?' queries Patrick Cormack MP. 'And of course the person in the pew voted in favour of this Measure,' countered Professor David McClean, the Synod member who steered the legislation through.

The Act of Synod had for a model Dr David Hope's plan for his then diocese of London, with the Bishop of Fulham, the Rt Revd John Klyberg (who retired in July 1996), assuming a non-geographical jurisdiction for parishes opposed to women priests which opted to enter it. Under the Act, the Archbishops have appointed three extra suffragans to be Provincial Episcopal Visitors (PEVs) – better known as 'Flying Bishops' – who are ombudsmen for the opposed.

They exercise episcopal ministry where it is needed, though in fact, many dioceses have the same sort of neighbourly arrangement as the one established in the capital by Dr Hope and the Bishop of Southwark, the Rt Revd Roy Williamson, with Bishop Williamson occasionally crossing the River Thames as the Bishop of London's commissary, to ordain women priests and act for 'pro' parishes in the Areas of those London bishops who are opposed.

In 1994, two archdeacons with impressive archdeaconly qualities were chosen to be flying bishops, although the expectation had been that there would be three: two for Canterbury, and one for York. In the southern province, the Rt Revd John Richards, the former Archdeacon of Exeter, was given the title of Bishop of Ebbsfleet; in the north, the Rt Revd John Gaisford, who was Archdeacon of Macclesfield, became Bishop of Beverley. Neither is the kind of Anglo-Catholic given to lace or incense – Prayer Book Catholic would be a better description – but both are sound traditionalists, both have chaired diocesan houses of clergy, and both are good diocesan men with records of service to the wider Church.

Pressure for the third PEV, who had been promised, but did not seem to be about to materialise, continued, and in 1995 the choice fell upon Canon Edwin Barnes, Principle of the Anglo-Catholic St Stephen's House theological college in Oxford. He is now Bishop of the new suffragan see of Richborough, in the southern province. His own view on the unacceptibility of women priests is firmly held, but he is a reconciliator, who worked hard to achieve a balance at St Stephen's House, where the views of the ordinands, who include women, are sharply divided, with 'pros' probably now in the majority. He yielded to demands for occasional celebrations of the eucharist by a woman, and agreed to invite in women priests from outside the college. His experience at holding together diverse opinions – something in which he believes the Church of England is developing great wisdom – will be useful, and he is just the man to reassure the Evangelical opposers, who had hoped for a third flying bishop from their own wing.

The Provincial Episcopal Visitors cannot function in any diocese without the consent of the diocesan bishop – an inevitable proviso, though there will be times when it adds to the complexities of their task.

Parishes which opt for alternative episcopal care will have passed two resolutions – A and B – which are built into the legislation. Resolution A says the parochial church council 'would not accept a woman as the minister who presides at or celebrates the holy communion or pronounces the absolution in the parish'. B resolves that the PCC 'would not accept a woman as the incumbent or priest-in-charge of the benefice or as a team vicar for the benefice'. Over 800 parishes have passed the resolutions, though in some cases only one of the two, for there are Evangelical parishes which might not object to a woman celebrant but could not consider a women as incumbent, because of their 'head of the house' principle, which limits the leadership role to men. Many PCCs which intend to keep to the spirit of the resolutions have not taken a vote on them for fear of making division in the parish sharper and more distressing than it already is.

The problems are not all on one side, for as the Dean of Worcester, the Very Revd Robert Jeffery, said in his preface to the 1994

Church of England Year Book: 'Those women who are ordained priest need to be aware that life will not change overnight. There is ample evidence from the Episcopal Church in America that being ordained priest does not necessarily guarantee a full ministry.'

According to the *Church Times*, the majority of the first thirty-two women priests ordained in Bristol had a good first year and enjoyed their new privileges to the full. Others of them were not so fortunate. Many are in chaplaincies rather than parishes; some have nowhere to go when they are required to move on from a first curacy, if only because they arrive in great numbers at a time when unemployment is beginning to bite throughout the hard-up Church of England. Canon Ian Hardaker, the clergy appointments adviser, is quoted as saying that when it comes to it, 'quite a few' parishes which are technically open to a woman incumbent do not, in fact, want one 'this time round'. And there seems to be no way round the deployment difficulties of at least 300 clergy couples, priests married to priests. A good move for one partner is liable to leave the other partner on the shelf.

'There will be many difficulties and prejudices to be overcome. A support and counselling system will be needed, as it is for all ministry,' wrote Dean Jeffery. Sally Barnes, who is married to Prebendary Donald Barnes, who was Vicar of St Peter's, Belsize Park, at Hampstead, in London, for sixteen years, would echo that. She is a founder-member of a London monitoring group called Watch (Women and the Church) set up to keep an eye on discrimination against women priests: 'to collect horror stories', she says. 'We're being careful, because it's not a witch hunt, in fact we are rejoicing, seeing good things happening up and down the country, in the parishes. It isn't all gloom and doom. But what has made us very distressed are the things happening within the boundaries of the legislation, which is rotten legislation, anyway. People in one parish where they wanted a woman priest and had one already chosen were then told they couldn't have her, and the living was suspended. There is now an anti-woman priest there instead.

'We are not talking about diversity. That mustn't be used as a cover for discrimination. Our curate, Claire Wilson, is very highly regarded, but the Bishop of Edmonton won't come here for anything sacramental now, so we had to get a retired bishop from Willesden for our confirmation, the Rt Revd Donald Arden, who was Archbishop of Central Africa, and that was very nice, because we had some African candidates. Most of us in Watch work in high-powered jobs where discrimination would be taken up, and I don't see why the church should be exempt. If I thought it was about theology, which I don't, I'd expect those opposed to be better behaved, but I think it's really because they don't like women. We're one of several monitoring groups in a number of dioceses and in the General Synod, and I expect we shall link together.'

The Revd Claire Wilson says, 'Sadly, it's entirely necessary, for reasons we put to the Bishop of London [then Dr David Hope] when we met him. Oh, well, he said he was sorry we felt that, but we told him of concrete examples of pressures being put on parishes. Discrimination happens even when, on the face of it, things look good for women; I know of dioceses where you'd think it would be different. Monitoring groups are going to be necessary right through the transition period to real acceptance. The powers that be must be kept on their toes.'

Mrs Barnes says Watch wants an inclusive and whole Church. Presumably, though the prospects never looked good, so did the powers that be who drafted the legislation and devised the Act of Synod. But the number of men leaving the stipendiary ministry for reasons other than retirement – which in recent years has run at just over 200 a year – almost doubled in 1994, though this was thought to be the peak year for resignations on the women priests issue. However, clergy who leave can claim compensation under the Financial Provisions Measure until ten years after the promulging of the canon on 22 February 1994, so more claims can be expected over the next few years.

Those who keep their convictions but want to stay on may have chosen the harder path. Damian Thompson was religious affairs correspondent of the *Daily Telegraph* when he wrote in *The Spec-*

tator: 'Anglo-Catholic clergy who talked grandly of leading their flocks to a new ecclesial home are discovering that many members of their congregations are happy to soften their opposition to women priests in return for an assurance that certain essentials – their parish church, the style of its services and, for the time being, the gender of its incumbent – remain unchanged. Faced with this, several highly public opponents of women priests have allowed themselves to be bought off with suffragan bishoprics and canonries; but most traditionalist clergy have stood their ground, if only because it is not clear what else they can do.'

Sometimes the opposers are more traditionalist than Catholic. Vivienne Goddard, a Lancashire member of Forward in Faith, said, 'Blackburn was one of the dioceses which voted against, but it wasn't a Catholic vote, there was more of a traditional feel. A lot of central churchmen here are against. We've had the Bishop in our parish, because we feel it's almost impossible to be out of communion with the diocesan bishop and stay. If we're going to stay we must fight from within, and you can't do that if you are an isolated congregation.'

Mrs Goddard is married to Canon John Goddard, the Team Rector of Ribbleton, who spoke against the Forward in Faith guidelines at the movement's 1994 national rally in London. Back in his parish, he said: 'The guidelines appear to those of us who want to stay to be so causing a barricade between those for and those against that the inevitable consequence will be the start of a third province, and that doesn't seem to me to be what maintaining the Catholic faith in the Church of England is all about.'

His parochial church council voted 18 to 3 for resolutions A and B, but it did not take up the option of choosing alternative episcopal care. 'I felt that if I had opted to be out of communion with my own Bishop, that would be the point at which I'd have to leave the Church of England. What we do need is more Catholic bishops. That is the challenge that faces the Church of England. It's not a matter of "No more Mr Nice Guy", as the Archdeacon of York has said, it's a commitment to stand where we stand for as long as we can, and that may, in the end, bring the victory. All I can say is,

I'm committed to this course of action so long as I feel with integrity that I can remain a Catholic in our Church. How can a totally secure Church witness to division in a broken world if it decides not to share that brokenness? Maybe the vocation for us is to share that brokenness. We may have something to say that no one else can.'

Dr David Hope's translation from London to be Archbishop of York in 1995 was a shot in the arm for many who never believed such a move could happen, even though in every other respect he was the obvious man for the job: a Primate who cannot accept the validity of women priests, though he keeps them and their work within his pastoral concern. He is a Yorkshireman with Yorkshire still in his everyday speech, going home to the North; a shrewd politician, with a priestly, down-to-earth and friendly persona, and the necessary lining of steel. As Archbishop, he does not ordain women priests or any priests at all, but only deacons, in which he follows the custom of his predecessor, Lord Habgood.

The Church in London was in a ferment at his going, because it seemed impossible to think of any diocesan bishop who could hold that divided diocese together. There were many Anglo-Catholic clergy who would have considered themselves out of communion with a bishop who had ordained women priests. On the other hand, seventy women priests and their supporters were ready to resist a bishop who appeared to undervalue their ministry. Any new bishop who was actively unfriendly to homosexual clergy would have been a disaster waiting to happen. Only Dr Hope could tell of the pressures which bear upon the man in London's hottest seat.

In the event, it was not a diocesan bishop who got the job, but – to the amazement of many, though not of those who had worked out the possibilities – the Area Bishop of Stepney, Richard Chartres, a member of the Bishop of London's staff, someone unable to accept the ministry of women priests, because, he says, it is not yet known whether or not they can be priests. At the age of forty-eight he was plucked out of a comparatively junior bishopric to be the third most senior cleric in the Church of England, a

role he can well support, for he is tall and imposing, more episcopal in appearance than most bishops on the bench, with a flam-
boyant style of dress and a reputation for being a bit of an
eccentric, in the way that bishops used to be. But he is well
earthed by his wife, Caroline, and their four young children.

Richard Chartres served a nine-year apprenticeship in matters
of state as domestic chaplain to Lord Runcie, at St Albans and at
Lambeth, before he became Vicar of St Stephen's, Rochester Row,
in Westminster. He has never ordained a woman priest, though he
has worked well with women priests in Stepney, and like the
Archbishop of York, he ordains only deacons. London, on the
whole, agreed that his appointment was the best hope for peace
in the diocese, though there was shock and anger among activists
campaigning for the universal acceptance of women priests, who
believed the move would turn London into an ecclesiastical ghetto.

On 11 November 1992, the day the General Synod passed the
legislation for the ordination of women to the priesthood, no one
could have imagined that within three years, two of the three most
important sees in England would be held by men from a part of
the Church which seemed to be heading for a rapid decline, and
was temporarily in the throes of something very close to despair.

But divisions are never the whole story in the Church of
England. At home in the parishes the issue of women priests soon
shrank in the face of more pressing concerns: money, mainly; the
maintenance of the precious church building, which it is said with
truth is what Church of England people really care about; and the
equally absorbing need to keep a priest in the parish by being able
to pay his stipend and contribute towards his pension.

The Archbishop of Canterbury, Dr George Carey, thought
women's ordination would be the biggest issue during his term of
office, but as he has told the General Synod, he was wrong about
that. The £800 million reduction in the Church Commissioners'
assets put it in the shade as far as the realities of everyday church
life were concerned.

Giving by church members is edging its way up towards an
average of something near £5 a week, which for most people is

still far short of the recommended 5 per cent of take-home pay; but the message is getting through. Mission and evangelism are the prime concerns of most parishes, partly because congregations must grow in order to survive, though there has to be more to it than that, because realists know that their best efforts will not bring many of the local population through the church door more than once in a while, however long the queues which wait to rush the stalls at jumble sales.

Church of England people genuinely want their neighbours to know that the church is there for them at times of need, for baptisms, marriages and funerals, which are often where evangelisation begins. The C of E is for everyone, especially those outside it; so there it has been, still is and will be, whether it is wanted or not.

CHAPTER THREE

Two or Three Together

Some villages still treat each other as if the Civil War was still being fought, even though they may share the same ordained leadership. (Country Way, *the magazine of the Arthur Rank Centre*)

IT MIGHT HAVE BEEN in Norfolk, or maybe in Gloucestershire, depending on who tells the tale. The legend of the parishes which refused to be joined together because they were on different sides in the war crops up in various parts of the Church of England, and in the story, the puzzled bishop eventually discovers that the war they mean is the war between cavaliers and roundheads. 'A thousand ages, in thy sight. . . .' You can still handle the canon balls Cromwell's soldiers lobbed into Lichfield Cathedral and see the traces of the damage they left behind them there and in many other places. It was not so very long ago. In any case, some old chestnuts not absolutely true in fact are true enough in essence to make them food for thought.

'It's quite serious,' says the Revd Jeremy Martineau, the Church of England's National Rural Officer. 'Certainly in the Fens you couldn't trust the folks in the next village, and look where it leads. Look what happened in Bosnia.'

Country congregations do not like sharing a vicar with an assortment of parishes incorporated into a multi-parish benefice. Unfortunately, they often have to, for stipendiary priests have been an endangered species in the countryside since the 1970s, when 'Sheffield' (the deployment policy devised by a working party chaired by the then Bishop of Sheffield) swept clergy out of the rural dioceses to increase the manpower in the cities. Country rectors and vicars, like village schools, shops, post offices and buses, are thin on the ground. Not that rural congregations take much notice when their incumbent tries to view the several parishes in his benefice as just one unit, for what they see is their own parish church, and they mean to stay in it.

This showed up when Jeremy Martineau carried out a rural survey involving incumbents in York, Worcester, Leicester and Chester, plus an archdeaconry apiece in Exeter and Ripon. Sixty-five per cent of the clergy in multi-parish benefices did not acknowledge the separate identity of individual parishes, but local people, on the other hand, did not acknowledge anything else.

Mr Martineau can sympathise with that, being a great believer in the depth of the worship when a handful of people gather together. 'With just two or three it's the most demanding kind of all. Of course it would be silly to preach to them, we need to learn something new; and they shouldn't sit scattered round the church. I came across one place where they took the pews out and kept a pile of stacking chairs by the door. You take one as you go in. I'd love to see where they sit.'

He was joint secretary to the Archbishops' Commission on Rural Areas (ACORA), which produced the *Faith in the Countryside* report in 1990, and he works in the Arthur Rank Centre, the churches' ecumenical base at the National Agricultural Centre, near Coventry . He is very much a countryman, and a villager, too, at home in Long Itchington, Warwickshire. 'For lay people,' he says, 'it's a question of "Where's your identity?" In no way would it be the name of the benefice they think of, that's only a description of the place of work of a clergyman.'

Yet there is a way of making things look reassuringly the same while people learn the art of sharing a vicar. Jeremy Martineau is one of a group which has presented the rural Church with the idea of borrowing a word that gardeners use: 'cloche' – a new way of describing a cluster of churches. Real cloches on allotments can be hard to put together, and they easily fall apart, which is one thing they have in common with parishes, but the diocesan rural officers cling to the thought that they are designed to promote growth.

'Church of England people do not travel to worship,' Jeremy says. 'Roman Catholics do, maybe because they have a high doctrine of the mass, or perhaps because their history has been that they have had to put themselves out, but for us, communion is a fellowship. Being in a cloche helps people to realise that there are some things they want to do in which they need to work with others, such as youth work, and community projects. For major resourcing, we need each other.'

A workbook for cloches emerged from the Arthur Rank Centre in 1995 with the title *Turning the Sod*, another horticultural inspiration which gave pleasure to the group which contributed to it. One member was the Revd Clive Thrower, a cloche incumbent in Derbyshire who doubles as rural officer for the diocese of Derby. 'There was resistance to the union of the benefice. Inevitably they see it as a loss, and my own researches have shown that parishes which don't have a resident vicar are significantly less strong than those who do. Some were minded to do things in a wider way, but most of the congregations see themselves in their congregation with me as their vicar.

'The Church wastes a lot of time considering the compatability of communities when the real question is whether the minister can run a communion of villages. Some antipathies go back to the Civil War. Often there are sociological difficulties. I've got one little farming community where they feel put down by the more well-heeled parts of the benefice, the people who've moved in and put a stop to any more development, so that our prices rocket. I'm in favour of cloches, of clusters. There's a sort of implicit policy of increasing the number of united communities to make it look as nearly in the old style as possible. My feeling is towards having a large cluster, served by a group of ministers. It makes it easier to organise.'

Prebendary Michael Hooper, the Rector and Rural Dean of Leominster, in Herefordshire, has become an expert on what is known as the minster model for running a cloche. It works like a wheel, with Leominster Abbey, the medieval priory which serves about 10,000 people as the only parish church in the town, at the centre, and the spokes leading off to about twenty little parishes in the countryside. 'You have to remember that in this part of the country the villages are very small indeed. We are talking of populations of about 150,' the Rector says. 'We've reached the point where we are reducing stipendiary clergy and opening up over twenty parishes.'

He is a member of the General Synod, a countryman brought up in rural Gloucestershire. 'I always thought I'd be in a rural area, because I understand rural people. They're not as daft as people think.' His background, Lampeter, and St Stephen's House, the Anglo-Catholic theological college in Oxford, is Catholic, but the ordination of women gives him no difficulty at all, and he says, 'I believe in the essentials, liturgically and sacramentally, without frills.'

The Leominster ministry team all live in the town, connected with the central church office by an internal telephone system, so that messages are sped through without delay. The lay leaders – about ten people responsible for baptism and marriage preparation, and a wider group of between twenty and thirty which meets to plan the worship – are scattered. There are also three licensed lay Readers, some of over 8,000 blue-gowned Readers in the Church of England, who are rigorously trained to preach, and to officiate at any services other than holy communion.

Prebendary Hooper has made one great discovery which renders the whole thing possible. 'It's no good asking villagers to rise up and go to a neighbouring church, but leaders seem quite acceptable across parish boundaries. You cannot move congregations about, but you can move leaders. As part of the evolution we need a really good working relationship between the churchwardens, the natural leaders in a parish, those who live there, and the others who live elsewhere. We have a Reader preparing for ordination who lives in one parish and is the accepted focus for ministry in two others where she does not live.

'We're breaking away from the model of the vicar being totally responsible for everything in the parish, and it seems theologically right. The difficulty of finding lay people to do things has disappeared for me since we started sharing ministry: lay people as co-workers rather than subordinates. I train them and let them get on with it. I was stopped in the street by someone who asked me about a baptism, and when I said I knew nothing about it, the reaction was "You *are* the Rector, aren't you?"

'Well, I think my role is oversight, but I do want to be involved in all areas of ministry. I still want to administer communion to the sick, and I still visit. Yet a pastoral care team can visit a hundred people in a week or two, and I couldn't do that in a year. They direct my energies. It's all a matter of not getting stuck for thirty years, but keeping people moving.'

But to find the real heart of Leominster's minster model ministry one would have to be in Leominster Abbey at seven o'clock on any weekday morning, when the stipendiary team fuels itself with half-an-hour of silent meditation, followed by morning prayer and holy communion. Michael Hooper says, 'I don't employ anybody who won't do that. It's the most important thing to do. A lot of lay people come as well, without anything being laid down to say they should. That's the engine room; and I still find it exciting after fourteen years. There are so many good things happening in the parishes, we had a thousand people following a Passion play on Good Friday; but that isn't the sort of thing people hear about the Church of England.'

On the other side of the country, in the similarly rural diocese of Lincoln, another kind of local ministry has been pioneered, which is spreading fast, though with variations in different dioceses. It is local non-stipendiary ministry (LNSM), and it raises questions not yet answered to the satisfaction of everyone. Who calls a person to local priesthood, God or the parochial church council? When a man or woman is 'locally ordained', to function only on one particular patch, is he or she still a priest outside the boundaries of the parish or group of parishes which did the calling?

In Lincoln, the process starts with local ministry teams of lay people being selected for a three-year training course by secret ballot in the PCC, which can give rise to a few diplomatic incidents.

Then at the end of the first year of training the parish can begin to consider whether any member of the team is being called to ordination; but what it must do is 'discern' God's call to an individual, the Lincoln scheme says. It must use its observance of a person's gifts and potential to aid its discernment that he or she is being called by God.

Brian Beves, a leading layman in Hereford, who has served on the General Synod, is someone who sees a bright future in LNSM schemes. 'Once you get them going they really do throw up people who want to be ordained, and in an ideal situation you would have a person/parson in every parish, selected by the parishioners. It's the problem of the very rural dioceses that if you look at the size of the population, if they were in a city, the whole population of Herefordshire would fit into a couple of London boroughs; and we have about 130 stipendiary clergy. The old people think they're terribly hard done by, but we try to persuade them that they are terribly lucky, in view of the population. The incomers do everything, and the locals don't do it themselves, and get very indignant at others doing it. But the ethos is changing from what lay people can do to help the clergy, to what the clergy can do to enable the lay people to be the Church. So the people who feel really threatened are the clergy, wondering, "What are we supposed to be doing?" This is the crux of it: if we empower the laity, where are the clergy?

'We are linked with a diocese in France, and there the number of clergy is far worse. A priest can have up to thirty parishes, and there is no possibility of him doing the job. The lay people just have to do everything. They whirl the sacrament round, and the parishes run themselves. Frenchmen say their women are *formidable*. But it's less complicated, because the clergy are actually not there. We have the few, but their burden is becoming unbearable.'

But local ministry also works without the calling out of ordinands, especially if there are retired clergy prepared to be part of a team. In the diocese of Ripon, Fountains Abbey, once the finest Cistercian monastery in Europe, and now a ruin carefully maintained by the National Trust, is having a new lease of active life as a focus for the Church of England. The Revd Tony Keddie's eleven villages – eight church buildings and a worship centre in a village hall – have taken its name: the Fountains Group of Parishes. The group covers 70 miles of North Yorkshire countryside with a total population of about 2500, and it functions with three local lay ministers, five lay Readers, two retired clergy, and Tony Keddie himself, who is the Rector and the sole stipendiary priest.

When the group was established, the perceived need was to lead worship, the Rector says. The clergy manage two eucharists apiece on any given Sunday; the rest of the team provides family services and morning and evening prayer. Training lay people to lead the worship is one of the priorities set out in *Faith in the Countryside*. Tony Keddie does not make heavy weather of the problems arising from eight church buildings. 'People care. A lot of love is lavished on the buildings. Villages have lost so much: schools amalgamated, police stations gone, even the pub in some places. The churches are the last marks left to them.'

The ruined Fountains Abbey, which has one covered area as insurance against the weather, is the base for a widening of the group's ministry. Services are held there. The town band from Ripon turns out on Good Friday and other occasions. And the Rector co-ordinates a team of twenty chaplains, lay and ordained, who provide what he calls 'a listening resource' for thousands of people who visit the abbey in the summer months. 'It's often easier to talk to a stranger. Many conversations start with something trivial, and before you know it, you're in deep waters. The chaplains enjoy the peace and beauty of the spot, and some of the clergy, retired and serving, use it as an opportunity for a quiet day. It's a well-loved spot, "where prayer has been valid", and there is an atmosphere about it that people seem able to detect.'

Not all the clergy can see themselves as managers of other people (of 'human resources', to use the technical term). 'That's certainly the way the Methodists have gone, but I'm not sure I want to go that way,' says the Revd Tom Thorp, Team Rector of Whitchurch in rural Buckinghamshire: eight churches, three stipendiary priests and three villages in his own care. 'I went in as a pastor. That's what my training was for. There are members of my PCC who are trained managers, and they should manage. They should manage the clergy.' He believes that as they are asked to give more, lay people will look for value for money. 'They'll ask how the vicar spends his time. They've never asked that before.'

His people know how he spends some of his. He is a volunteer fireman, the leader of the crew which mans the local fire engine. The four minutes allowed to get from church or vicarage to the fire station is no problem to a marathon runner and all-round sportsman, which he is, and if the alarm goes during a service they wait with fair good nature until he comes back. Blazing haystacks account for most of the fire calls, but his crew works in a bad area for road accidents, and those are the times of tragedy when being there becomes an extension of his ministry. As chaplain to the Buckinghamshire Fire Service he tries, with other brigade chaplains, to alter the official attitude in the service, which he says leaves a lot to be desired, for it leans to the view that if firefighters need counselling to help them deal with distress and trauma, they must be too soft for the job. That is one priest's foothold among people in his area who would probably seldom be found in church.

Tom Thorp believes, like all country priests, that the more that is taken away from the villages, the harder the rural Church has to try to put something back. 'If the shop shuts one hopes that something else will emerge, but it takes a long time. One village here where the shop closed was like a ghost village. No one had a reason to go out. No one was walking in the streets. People went to town for their shopping. It was quite devastating; people who don't live in villages haven't any idea. We tried coffee mornings, but it wasn't the same, and it was two years before people began to say, "I could just go for a walk." The village association started to grow and be better supported. People realise that community doesn't just happen, and the Church has a great part to play in this.'

The Church is playing the part to the full in places where the parish church has started a village shop and post office of its own, sometimes in part of the church building. At Stanton-by-Dale, in Derbyshire, the Revd Ian Gooding has done it by converting an old air-raid shelter in the playground of a former school, which is now a church centre, with a house attached for the postmistress (paid by the Post Office) who also looks after the shop with the help of volunteers. The shop is open six mornings a week, with a wide range of groceries and other goods, and plenty of parking space. His problem now is the need for bigger premises.

Increasingly, the rural Church is applying itself to the other big issue in villages: the lack of houses which young locals can afford. Incomers bring a good deal, but they take a lot away, including the homes from which villagers' children have been ruled out by inflated prices. Council houses, bought when the option to buy was offered, have been sold on. A number of dioceses have followed the example of Hereford by setting aside some of their glebe land for affordable local housing. Townees might harbour pipe dreams about the country, which to them, as *Faith in the Countryside* says, 'still seems reassuringly stable, a refuge from the thrust of technology and the tough realities of work and competition in the cities'. That is only how it looks on the surface.

The report warns: 'This view of the rural idyll has the power of myth. But too often it leads us to feed fantasies and avoid facing up to what is really happening.' The high rate of suicide among farmers is a chilling reminder of that. The agricultural chaplains and the Arthur Rank Centre have been working with the Samaritans, the Citizens Advice Bureaux and Christian lay people to set up rural helplines for those who come to believe that their problems are insoluble.

Joining forces with other denominations happens more often in the rural dioceses, where ecumenism is often a matter of practicality. Among 13,000 Church of England parishes there are about 750 local ecumenical projects, known as LEPs, where the congregation and ministry is shared with other churches. Earlier question marks which hung over them have disappeared since the General Synod found it prudent to legalise what was already going on to most people's satisfaction in many places.

Nonconformist churches have had to pull out of some areas, leaving the parish church as the only place of worship, and their people may then become part of the Anglican congregation. When that happens, although Methodists, Baptists or United Reformed Church members will still belong to their own churches, they can be fully integrated, and serve on parochial church councils.

It is not always an everyday story of country folk in the rural parishes. Even BBC Radio 4's 'The Archers', in Ambridge, have had to put up with changes, like everyone else, and Jeremy Martineau, who is religious adviser to the programme, has been wanting to put a local ministry team in place there for a long time. When Ambridge, like so many other villages, lost its full-time stipendiary incumbent, he appointed Robin the vet, an NSM (non-stipendiary minister), but not to be confused with LNSMs.

There are about 1500 NSMs, usually professional or business people with secular careers to pursue, and back in the 1970s they were felt to be the cavalry coming to the rescue of the Church's shrinking ministry, but the scheme has not worked out in that way. An unexpectedly high number of them began to filter across to the stipendiary ministry, and of those who did not cross the line, about half have their hearts in the parishes. The rest have always seen themselves as lawyers, doctors, bank managers, engineers – almost anything one can think of – who are ordained: 'doing theology on the work front', they say; and they do not necessarily help out in church on Sundays, because that is not where they function. They are now called MSEs, ministers in secular employment. The ones who regard their non-stipendiary ministry as a back-up to the parochial clergy are still NSMs.

The Archers seemed happy enough with Robin the vet, though he would not have suited everyone, in Ambridge or anywhere else, but they will probably know by now that worse can befall. And farming people are not as visible in the country as they used to be. In the Cambridgeshire flatlands, near St Neots, in the diocese of Ely, where vast skies reach down to an endless landscape, and the sunsets are of indescribable splendour, the Revd Tim Marks says that what he has there is an urban ministry in the country.

Apart from half-a-dozen tiny congregations of country people hanging on in their medieval churches, he has villages filling up with affluent, young, two-car families whose indifference to the Church is total, and he must minister to them, too.

'If your church was culturally out of step you'd expect that you had to – painfully, over a period of time – get it into step. But sometimes it's not possible for an older congregation to change. I have those who stick to the 1956 *Ancient and Modern*, because "That's the one we saved up for." To impose on them family services and songs of fellowship – it's going to screw them up, so I've had to build up a congregation of people who wanted to worship differently in a different place at a different time. It's a different vision.

'If you are looking after twelve people in the country the vision is to keep them together. What they're doing is wonderful; they are meeting together every Sunday to worship, and take it into their lives. But reaching out to young parents who are floundering about with no spiritual vocabulary to help them – invite them to come to church and you might as well invite them to come to China. I keep both the evangelising, and the befriending which comes before it, away from parish worship.

'There's a Thursday morning meeting for under-fives and mums, and a third will come to the rectory the next week while I talk about prayer and the kids play. Some come to nothing else other than that, because it would be a big thing to come to a family service. It would mean the wife saying to her husband, "I've got a spiritual interest"; and that's where you find that the marriage comes first. The Church seems quite threatening to a lot of the guys around. It questions all the values of the home, and they don't like it.'

Tim says, 'Everyone who doesn't come to church calls me Tim, and that would be true for just about all under seventy, but the older ones find it hard not to call me Sir, or Mr Marks, because they used to regard the vicar as a sort of spiritual squire. We had an old lady who was very ill for two years, and at first I was just too much for her, so she stopped coming to church. She was quite crabby and hostile; she always called me Sir. In hospital, she mellowed. I was sitting talking to her (by this time we were holding hands), and to someone who came along she said, "I don't think you've met my vicar, the Revd Marks – or as I call him now, Tim." '

When Tim greeted the congregation with 'Happy Easter!' at a big family service, the response that came back to him was 'Cheers!' He says: 'It was like a whole community making the responses it felt able to make. We've had about twenty people come to faith over two-and-a-half years, and some were real conversions. Those who come to the agnostics' workshop usually say after about six weeks, "I believe this." A big macho man arrived at the rectory one night, afraid of what he might be tempted to do to some difficult neighbours; but belligerence faded as he let off steam. We talked, and when he left, he put down a case of lager, saying, "That's for the time."

'The new Christians are all good givers, they cough up about £2000 a year to help other parishes with their quotas. When you take little Eltisley, twelve people, and a quota of £3800 a year, it's ridiculous. There's too much emphasis on money. This is a pioneer mission situation.'

Paying the quota is not the only struggle which goes on in the country. The fate of the big and often beautiful old rectories and vicarages has been fought over since the 1960s, when the Church began to speed up a process of selling them off to wealthy incomers, and replacing them with new houses which were often inadequate for their purpose and in constant need of expensive repairs. Some angry parishioners in Suffolk have launched a group called Save Our Parsonages* which keeps a register of historic parsonages all over the country not yet sold. According to the Rural Theology Association, which supports the campaign, that is only 15 per cent in Hereford, 20 per cent in Peterborough, 25 per cent in Oxford, and in other dioceses more – or less.

Another uncivil war is about bats, those little furry mammals which make nature-lovers ecstatic and drive volunteer church

---

* Bulmer Tye House, near Sudbury, Suffolk CO10 7ED

cleaners to distraction. The fourteen British species of bats are laughing since the Wildlife and Countryside Act secured their future as sitting tenants, because not even the keenest members of the anti-bat wing of the Church want to pay £1000 for destroying their habitat. The Movement Against Bats in Churches (Mabic), founded by Catherine Ward, the Rector's wife at Bale, near Fakenham, in Norfolk, would like a change in the law, to exclude churches from the Act, but that is unlikely to happen, for the pro-bat wing is supported by English Nature, the government nature conservation agency, and the Bat Conservation Trust. The supporters of Mabic clean on in frustrated fury, covering the altar and the carpets with plastic sheeting, bewailing the droppings which fall on people's heads, and bat urine which takes the varnish off the pews and dents the brasses.

'The first time I saw it I thought someone had been in with a watering-can,' says a woman churchwarden in Norfolk. 'I've done so much, worked so hard . . . well, I wouldn't want it in my house, why do they want it in God's house? How would they like to be sitting watching television and have something go plop on their head?'

Yet the Revd Andrew Good, not far away, at Spixworth, delights in the flock of maternal pipistrelle bats, which roost in his church roof. He invites small groups of bat enthusiasts to watch them gliding and swooping about the church for two hours at dusk, before they go out to feed, and as the visitors contribute to the upkeep of the building, the parishioners love the bats, too. The Rector says, 'The bats seem to be communicating, socialising and having fun, giving the little ones a safe place to play. Sometimes I find a baby bat in the morning, dehydrated and suffering from hypothermia, then I give it water on my finger, put it in a woollen bag, and take it to a parishioner who hangs it in her airing cupboard until it recovers.'

Bats seem to bring blessings to parishes which consider their comfort. When the thatched church of St Lawrence, at South Cove, in Suffolk, had its roof renewed (using bat-friendly materials) the PCC decided to leave holes between the underside of the thatch and the roof-boards: a series of front-doors for the church's colony of brown long-eared bats. An estimate of £54,000 for the repair and restoration of the church presented the tiny village with a challenge that seemed impossible to meet, in spite of its energetic fundraising; but bat-power came to the rescue. The money rolled in from bat enthusiasts everywhere, even in the USA, where the L.C. and Mary Scraggs Foundation backed the project to the tune of $10,000. South Cove won the 1994 Suffolk Architects Association Craftsmanship Award out of 420 entries; the electoral roll increased from seven to twenty; and the total amount of money raised was £61,800.

The bat war goes on, but English Heritage has heard the cries of Mabic and has commissioned an investigation to look at the extent of the problem and to put forward some possible solutions. Perhaps they will come up with something more sophisticated than a stuffed owl sitting on the window-sill, which country people say used to work all right in the old days – like a lot of other things now gone from the rural scene.

CHAPTER FOUR

Dedicated Cities

All that dedicated city
Dearly loved by God on high . . .
(Office hymn, seventh century, translated by J. M. Neale)

IMAGINE MISS MARPLE, picking her way through the recently demolished but rapidly regenerating streets of Hulme, in Manchester's Moss Side, quelling rude youths with a look. Why one should imagine Agatha Christie's spinster-detective in such an unlikely scenario, so far from the village of St Mary Mead, and apparently so unlike it, will emerge only after a conversation with a priest from Manchester who is now the Dean of Ripon, the Very Revd John Methuen. It is nothing to do with the fifty break-ins at the rectory, which were not mysterious but only too predictable.

Before he went to Ripon in autumn 1995, John Methuen was Rector of The Ascension, Hulme, for twelve years, in the front line of inner-city ministry. The Ascension was famous, some would say notorious, between the end of 1986 and the beginning of 1989, because for the whole of that time Fr Methuen and his congregation gave sanctuary there to an asylum-seeker from Sri Lanka, Viraj Mendes, who was eventually deported to face the welcome which awaited him in his own country. 'It took a year to get him out of Sri Lanka again, and during that time there were three attempts on his life.' Viraj and his wife, a Manchester woman whom he met while he was in sanctuary and married in Sri Lanka, now live in Germany.

'Urban regeneration' – making the wilderness blossom – has been John Methuen's watchword, and by the time he was preparing to go to Ripon, three-quarters of his parish was demolished, the other quarter was refurbished, and he was one of the directors of

Hulme Regeneration Ltd, which works with a budget of £60 million a year, delivering Hulme's share of development under the Government's City Challenge scheme. He started the ball rolling with the aid of the Church Urban Fund, which was set up in 1987 on the recommendation of *Faith in the City*, the report of the Archbishops' Commission on Urban Priority Areas (UPAs). The Fund presented a huge challenge to church people in all the dioceses, who were asked to raise £18 million of new money to bring the run-down inner cities back to life.

So how essential is the Church's involvement in what the clergy always call 'the community', popular churchspeak for the whole unchurched neighbourhood which rarely sees the inside of the church building? 'Well, I think that when people ask me that question,' says Dean Methuen, 'I refer to the legendary St Mary Mead, the village where Miss Marple lives, and that's very much the sort of archetypal English village, though whether of course any such village has existed or does exist today . . . But if you've got that sort of image in your mind – the village has the little shop, the school, the tea-room, the pub and the parish church, and all of them integrate together, so that you'll go into the pub, and you'll find a big jar for collecting for the church roof repair fund. Or if you go to the school's annual concert, the compere will be the vicar; and he'll be the chairman when all of them combine in a petition to make sure the motorway is routed a long way from the village – those sorts of things. The involvement of the church in the life of the community is quite normal in those circumstances, and regarded as part of the English scene.

'Now I regard the style of ministry The Ascension is trying to do as an urban equivalent of that; so what I believe us to be doing is something really very traditional, only of course the issues are not quite the same in human Moss Side as they are in St Mary Mead. Our issues, all that concern people here, are housing, employment and social justice, but they're just as much community issues in Hulme as they are in St Mary Mead. When you listen to Conservative politicians, they would tend to say, "Oh, that's the Church being political", in the one and not in the other, which in my opinion is grossly illogical.

'I feel that this goes back really to the nature of the English parochial system, that for a thousand years in this country, every square foot of the land has been in somebody or other's parish, and the Church has always said, no doubt a bit arrogantly, I suppose, that it has taken responsibility for everybody and everything that goes on within the boundaries of the parish. If you take that seriously, that concept of parochial ministry, which I do, then it's all very well for John Wesley to say the world is his parish, but frankly, we've got enough to do in one small parish here, let alone the whole world.'

Life can be hazardous and lonely for the clergy of the inner cities, the only middle-class people who stay on the scene as soft targets round the clock. 'Doctors, teachers and social workers tend to come in on a daily basis and do good to Hulme. It's only the clergy who actually live in the inner cities, and I think that gives the clergy a certain amount of street credibility that other middle-class professionals don't have to the same extent. But the picture is changing with the Hulme regeneration, and the whole place is getting much more integrated back into the life of the city as a whole.'

The fiftieth break-in at The Ascension rectory, was 'celebrated' well before John Methuen's appointment to the Deanery of Ripon. 'After a bit you lose all that sense of rape and pollution people get when they're burgled. When my children were small, in our first six months here, it got to the point when they said, "What have they got this time, Daddy?"' After his new job was announced: 'One of my friends rather unkindly sent me a "Best wishes on your retirement" card, but at the age of forty-seven I think there's still a little bit left.

'But to return to the parochial system, it is because the Church of England is established, and all that, but it is also in my view fundamental to the nature of the gospel that the Christian God is a God who comes here, because he's an incarnate God, and that has huge implications, for all sorts of things of course, but one thing it does mean is that human life and life on earth – but especially human life – is of absolute significance to God. In fact the message, the doctrine of the Ascension, and I mean now *the* Ascension rather than the church, means that humanity and the incarnateness of God is something eternal – you know, those old Ascension hymns, about "Man with God is on the throne" – that humanity is taken up into the Godhead, that Christ never loses his humanity, that God comes here, rolls up his sleeves and gets his hands dirty, and becomes one of us, so that man might become divine. The doctrine of the Incarnation is actually what I feel lies behind the parochial system, or should; and therefore if that is the sort of God we have, then that is what the Church's ministry, which seeks to serve that God, should be like, too.'

The same theology is behind one thousand parish projects which have received grants from the Church Urban Fund: there is such a variety that one can only pick some out with a pin. A lot of people thought the targets for the dioceses, a total of £18 million, were set too high. 'Not being a Church of England man, I said "They'll never do it." Who could have thought it?' says Chris Hallam, a Methodist church treasurer from the High Wycombe circuit who is the fund's field officer, the man on the ground who pays the initial visit and helps the parish put its case to the grants committee. The dioceses raised not £18 million but £20 million.

Canon John Stanley, of Liverpool, who chaired the grants committee for three-and-a-half years, used to set aside three or four days before each meeting just to read the applications. 'It took a lot of time. I reckon about a month each year. Even though we had an annual sum of £2.5 million to distribute, it was so little when we were being asked for twice and sometimes three times that amount.' He has described his visit to a project for women with drink problems, some of whom had been out on the streets. 'As I listened and heard those stories told with simplicity and sincerity and such honesty, I felt that this was holy ground. Here was a group of women whom the Church had touched. It had helped to give them a sense of dignity and worth, and helped them start to take control of their own lives. The application we had read had been given a human face. It was a deeply moving experience. The gospel changes people.'

Nic Frances, who describes himself as a former Thatcherite stockbroker, says that the gospel has certainly changed him, which, he explains, is why he is now a long way from the City of London in more senses than one, presiding over the Furniture Resource Centre in Liverpool, a 'poverty and unemployment' project started off and topped up by Church Urban Fund grants. 'Over our first six years we furnished ten thousand homes, free of charge. Now it's illegal to give out foam furniture, but we repair cookers and fridges and sent them out by a delivery service for a small charge. Councils can phone us and we deliver whole sets of new furniture, and they get the money back over a period from housing benefit.'

He blames reduced taxes and decreased Government spending for the poverty he sees every day, yet: 'I was a strong advocate of Thatcher policies. Then I did some personal development work in my life, I was selling stocks and shares, and I realised that all I was saying about choice was a lie. I remember Bishop David Jenkins saying that choice only means something when it's a choice for good; choice itself is nothing of value. And I was getting choices because I had the money. Mine came from the dealings on the Stock Exchange which meant that firms were going bankrupt and putting people off. For me, regardless of how much time or money I gave, I never quite felt the charity, the love, that would remove the taste of injustice from my mouth.'

Nic Frances says, 'I couldn't stay in London, with all my friends telling me not to worry, and anyway, the style of Liverpool is what I enjoy.' By now he is the Revd Nic Frances. He was ordained as a non-stipendiary minister at Petertide 1995, to continue his work at the Furniture Resource Centre.

In west London, the Revd John Wheeler, Vicar of St Saviour's with St Mary's, Hammersmith, can remember a time when life was comparatively ordinary. 'We were like any other vicarage in the country, where you get knocks on the door from people who are hungry, who are lost, needing help.' It is a Tuesday morning;

Tuesday is Listening Day in the Upper Room, a name describing
part of the half of his church which is divided off for 'community
purposes', though in this case something like 'human happiness'
would be a better way of putting it.

The Upper Room is also the name of the ecumenical project
based at St Saviour's, backed by the Church Urban Fund and
'founded on the Christian imperative to love and support our
neighbour,' says the annual report. On this day the neighbours are
the regular customers, men and women who sleep rough, the
persistently jokey ones together at one table, the rest sitting
quietly, reading papers, drinking coffee, working through piles of
breakfast toast, chatting with two Roman Catholic nuns and a
friendly looking church lady from the vicar's former parish, who
have come to listen to the stories of those who like to tell them.
A chiropodist awaits a call; at other times there is a nurse's clinic;
and someone from the Job Centre is there, to discuss courses that
just might set someone on the way back to work.

'We made porridge as well this morning, by request. Sometimes
we boil eggs, too,' says Brenda Wheeler, wife of the vicar and part-
time administrator of the project. The exciting times, she says, are
when things arrive from Prêt à Manger, collected and delivered by
Crisis, the charity for the homeless, as one of its services. Prêt à
Manger is a super-smart London chain of takeaways which special-
ise in sandwiches and pastries with exotic fillings, and are fortu-
nately very fussy about their sell-by dates.

'His shoes are falling apart,' the vicar says quietly to his wife,
coming away from one conversation. She keeps a stock of clothes
and shoes behind the door marked 'Clothes Shop'. There is a small
charge, says John Wheeler, 'otherwise some bright spark would
set up a stall down the road'.

Brenda Wheeler organises her forty-five volunteers – spotless
toilets, spotless everything, are essential to the smooth running of
the place – and she plans and shops for the 12,000 meals the
Upper Room serves every year: soup and sandwiches basically,
and two-course dinners on Sundays. The mothers and children
have properly balanced meals, 'so they're not eating crisps and

burgers every day of the week,' says John. Brenda ran the Play and Learn group for single mothers and their children until a grant provided two trained workers, and the project also has a full-time salaried developer for fundraising, for the Upper Room is one of the projects which grew too big for the parish. It has its own management committee, with the vicar, who is the chaplain, among the directors.

He looks back to the knocks on the vicarage door in the 1980s. 'Our children were very good about making tea and sandwiches. Then we began to regularise it, to say that people should come between certain hours; and we cleared the garage, put in benches, so that they could sit and eat out of the rain.' The Wheelers have six children, three of them adopted, from ethnic groups, and John believes that racism is ingrained in the English character. 'Look at what we used to read as children. When I sign a passport photo for a black person there is always a check call from the authorities. With a white person, never.'

When the garage became crowded, 'I gave the photographic studio in our hall six months' notice, and told the congregation it would be used for the most needy and deprived people in the community. All but one agreed, even though it meant we lost a major source of income. I told them to increase their stewardship for the next six months, and they did. It has used a lot of energy, not just money, though we have to raise £65,000 a year; but I lost my church treasurer – he's treasurer here now – and my best secretary, because they do it for the Upper Room. It's a very local thing.

'We've had two suicides and a murder over the past two years, though not on the premises, and some horrible things, like a man with gangrene, who lost his leg. They could be me, who has taken a wrong turning somewhere, struggling to get back to the society which is so intolerant of poverty, of failure. As a charity, we can't be politicised, but we have to be aware of the society in which we live. The trouble is, you get an alcoholic trying to dry out, he's reached the depths, the only people he can relate to are other alcoholics, and if he manages to pull himself out, he's left with no friends at all. Some people say, "They could buy steak if they didn't buy booze." I can't control their behaviour in the park, if they throw beer cans, but opposition usually comes through fear of the unknown. The support is there among individuals, but it's something people would rather not know. We did have a shooting, not by one of the members, but by someone who took exception to a member, and we've had windows smashed, just through spleen; but we did all this in consultation with the neighbours, the school, the nursery, and we've had no complaints.

'Half the volunteers are from the congregation and half from other churches. The confirmation classes from the Roman Catholic church use it as part of their preparation, and the Society of St Vincent de Paul is one of our main supporters. We don't preach, and we've only one rule: no alcohol on the premises, and I think we've got the best behaviour standard of anywhere like this I know. Of course we're putting on sticking plaster, as it was necessary to pour oil into the wounds on the road to Jericho; allowing a situation to continue, because, in a way, people can go on. It's just part of the pastoral outreach of a church.'

So it all comes down to the parishes. 'People speak supportively, but they don't want to see it. They don't want it where they are,' says the Revd Derek White, the Bishop of London's Chaplain to the Homeless. 'You have to go somewhere where people are sympathetic, and if they're not, forget it, because the attitude is, "They should get their act together and stop being layabouts" and that is the attitude of people in and out of the Church. There is no co-ordinated approach to homelessness by the Church, it's all left to individual parishes.'

A blue door next to an old-fashioned shoe-repair shop in London's Drury Lane has a modest slot by one of the bells which says simply 'Basement office', and that is where he is, down below, his conversations punctuated by the merry tapping and occasional loud bangs from the cobbler upstairs. His office is one of the few places in London where you still find ashtrays.

Fr White looks an unlikely Anglo-Catholic priest, though he is one, and has been for over twenty years. The church of St Mary le Strand was added to his charge in 1995. He sports a moustache, very unusual in the Southern Province, not so much so in the North, and he still bears the stamp of a Church Army officer, for he has been one for forty years – officially, you could call him Captain – but then, he says, the Church Army, founded by Prebendary Wilson Carlile in 1882, had a wider sweep when he joined in 1956. It has about 400 officers, trained evangelists working in areas of need, especially in the inner cities.

'Yes, I went in as an Anglo-Catholic, it wasn't a contradictory thing then, because in the old days the Church Army had churchmanship right across the board. Now it's Evangelical and left-wingy, but Wilson Carlile said he wouldn't become the first Chief Secretary unless it represented the whole breadth of traditions in the Church, and that was true up to about fifteen years ago. It's become very clappy-happy. You look back with a bit of nostalgia, but you know, you didn't have to justify yourself as you sometimes do today. I suppose I'm an old-fashioned Tractarian. I'm glad I came in when I did, my heart bleeds for young priests. It's all going to take about forty years for things to settle down.'

As Chaplain to the Homeless in London, he says his task is purely pastoral. 'They wouldn't expect a chaplain at a hospital to perform neurological surgery. My job description is to provide pastoral care for the homeless people and those who work among them; the pressures are tremendous on both. They want to talk to someone who won't involve them in a quick-fix solution. We befriend, and they talk quite openly, because they know we aren't going to come at them with the social work handbook.

'I'm amazed how many people I see sleeping in doorways when I walk along the Strand, because one is told they have been moved, and the numbers reduced; but although they're not as obvious as they used to be, they are still there. So many people consider that the problem with these people is that they're homeless, but that is not the whole of it. I see some I know who have been on the streets for eighteen years, and there are new ones coming up the ladder to take the place of the older people who've moved out. Half of those on the streets have been in care, and there are broken marriages, broken homes, but care is the most frequent common denominator.

'One thing we desperately need is somewhere they can go in and have two or three nights, and not be social-workered up to the eyeballs. Some people want to be left alone. People know when they've had enough of their life-style. When they're not well, then they take themselves off for a few days respite, but those places are few and far between now that the big hostels have been closed. That was a mistake; but they were very run-down, and refurbishment was too expensive. Then there are those rehoused in flats, who can't budget, can't manage money. They spend three or four days in the flat and the money runs out before the fortnight is up for the next payment, so they're on the streets again. Some just can't bear to be within four walls. But it's been going on for at least a hundred years round here.

'At the beginning of the century the Church Army had tents in the Strand to accommodate homeless people, financed by King Edward, because Queen Alexandra was a great supporter of Wilson Carlile, our founder, but there is no organisation in the Church to co-ordinate it now. The Church Army pioneered these things before the Salvation Army did. The first Church Army hostel was in 1888, and the men got a job of work to do, a meal, a bed and a sermon. The Church Army did it for eighty or ninety years, it was the social outreach arm of the Church, but it has diminished its role and most of the organisations that do it now are secular: but the Church started so many of those things. Centrepoint was started at St Anne's, Soho, but it's now completely secular. Twenty years on, the kind of provision in the way of day care is what we pioneered in the 1970s. There are outreach workers everywhere on the streets now, but it was my idea in 1978.

'One of the most important roles of a baptised person, of any Christian, is to love one's neighbour as one's self, and it's so simple, we know it so well, that we forget it. It's the same with the homeless, accepting them as they are, loving them as they are, so that they may become what God intended them to be. If we don't do it, no one else will. We have to see that what we do has the hallmark of Christ on it, and the food, the clothes we give, those are the outward and visible signs of that inward and spiritual grace. I hope to be perfected myself, one day, and if I love them enough, they will be perfected, too. We must be a constant factor, in whom there is no variableness, no turning, so that they can say, "Oh, it's Father Derek, he's always around." Then even if they say, "Sod off," it doesn't matter, just so long as they know I'm there.'

That goes for the Church of England, too. Being there is the name of the game, and sometimes it brings its rewards, though it may take a crisis to awaken the rest of the population to the Church's desire to stand alongside the people. It happened in the coalfield parishes at the time of the pit closures, in the dioceses of Sheffield, Wakefield, Durham and Southwell, in places so bereaved by the loss of a whole way of life that the sense of desolation was almost tangible. The people there were used to sudden death, their history had prepared them for the ever-present threat of accidental disaster, but not for the kind of death where courage and stoicism could no longer see them through, and where no one any longer had the heart to say, 'Life must go on.'

The parish clergy were there then, right at the pit gates, fulminating, comforting, offering the opportunity to pray as people stood with the miners' wives who camped outside when closure was imminent. They saw the local businesses struggle and give up as the loss of pay packets went down the line. They felt the humiliation of macho men pushing prams while their wives took part-timing cleaning jobs, and they dealt as best they could with the inevitable domestic rows brought on by stress and fear for the future. They showed, as Bishop David Lunn of Sheffield said at the time, that one man and his family living in one house – the vicarage – could save a whole community from despair.

The bishops of the coalfields carried on the battle in London, in the House of Lords, and at a massive miners' rally in Parliament Square. And it made a difference. 'Yes, I've been saying that it did, because the Government had to review its plan, to go back and . think again,' says the Revd Tony Attwood, who was Coalfields

Chaplain in Sheffield through it all until he moved in the autumn of 1995 to head the Teesside Industrial Mission in the diocese of Durham. When he arrived in Sheffield in 1986, two years after the coal strike, there were twenty-six coal-mines in South Yorkshire, employing 26,000 men. As he left, there were four mines, with jobs for only 5 per cent of the former workforce. 'But instead of two pits we've got four; we were able to see miners taking home wages for some months more, a year, in some cases, which meant there was more money going into the community as well.

'The Bishop's Council happened to be meeting the day Mr Heseltine announced his plan for closures, and a petition was launched from there, which got between 60,000 and 70,000 signatures in a week. I think people have a higher regard for the Church now; the local media interest has grown. I'm aware that it's all very much a collaborative effort, a partnership of interests, the churches together, people like me and those at congregational level, lay and ordained. When the Church makes its plans for evangelism the church members can say, "We've a long-standing commitment in these areas, for themselves, not for the good of the Church, but the community." We can stand on our own feet in terms of working for people and doing it for God, as well as proclaiming the gospel.'

When young Asian rioters caused havoc in the Manningham area of Bradford in June 1995, the Bishop and the Manningham clergy were out on the streets, treading the broken glass, talking and listening. 'Mostly it was listening to the anger and frustration pouring out. As much as anything, it was being there,' said the Bishop of Bradford, the Rt Revd David Smith. 'We wanted to show that we were concerned for the whole city, not least those whose shops were smashed and their businesses ruined, and all those of any religion who live in terror of violence.'

Lifting up an inner-city parish with nothing much left of its past and no community spirit to hold it together is a different challenge. There must be more than one way of meeting it; more than one might succeed. A priest could risk an early breakdown by driving himself into a frenzy of activity; he could soldier on with very little going for him, waiting and hoping; or he could try what Dr John Sentamu of the General Synod decided to do at Holy Trinity, Tulse Hill, in south London, when he went there in 1983. 'I started with nine months of prayer, with a group of three people, on Wednesday mornings, leading them into new ways of worship that were fresh. Then the time came when some musicians moved into the parish . . .'

Prayer and music, but also the ebullient personality of John Sentamu, who comes from Uganda, where he was a High Court judge. He is a powerful evangelist. When he speaks in the General Synod, he gathers momentum as he goes, and rocks the whole assembly. Not everyone could do it his way. But when he left to be Bishop of Stepney, there were between 400 and 500 people in church on Sundays, and a parish centre which cost £1.6 million. 'And how it happened, I really don't know,' he says. 'Some of the money came from very poor people. Some of them are actually tithing from income support.'

There are about ninety-two black clergy in the Church of England. Dr Sentamu chairs the General Synod's Committee for Black Anglican Concerns, which in 1994 produced a report on black Anglican membership of the Church of England in the 1990s, *How We Stand*, compiled from a 60 per cent response which represented 7374 parishes. Some parishes in London would die without their almost entirely black congregations, but then in the capital, the dioceses of London and Southwark, on either side of the River Thames, have almost half the total number of black Anglicans in the country who go to church on Sundays.

Outside London and Birmingham, black Anglicans are unevenly dotted about, which may account for the feeling that they are under-represented on PCCs and deanery and diocesan synods. Anyone who goes to a service for the swearing-in of church-wardens in London would think that black churchwardens abound, because in the capital, they do: 61 in London, 55 in Southwark. In the country as a whole the survey showed 213. There were 39 black Readers, 17 black Church Army officers, 1654 black PCC members, 237 black deanery synod members, and 38 on diocesan synods. At the last General Synod elections, 13 black candidates were successful out of 26 who stood: 13 out of a total membership of about 570.

A booklet which was produced by diocesan *Faith in the City* link officers for church people with no first-hand experience of Urban Priority Areas speaks of 'the corporate sinfulness' that leaves some 'powerless'. Power, or rather powerlessness, is another expression which, like 'the community', always comes up in Church debates and discussions, and as with many true sentiments often repeated, it can begin to sound dreary. The human interest lies in the things which are actually being done to change the picture, and the booklet *Discovering Faith in the City*, by Canon Robert Langley of Newcastle Cathedral, and others, tells of some of them. A group of mothers and children from one UPA parish went to spend the middle of the week in the homes of the better-off partner parish. 'For them it was a release from the pressure and tension of their estate; for the receivers there was learning, not only about life in a UPA, but from the courage and endurance of the mothers.' In a partnership, givers must be takers too. There was also an alluringly practical idea, when one UPA parish held its jumble sale in the up-market partner parish, and raised four times as much money as usual.

Diocesan link schemes, perhaps north with south, start off with some irresistible stereotyping. When Guildford and Sheffield began one, and some Sheffield people went to stay in Surrey, at least one hostess admitted later that she had expected to open her front door to a cloth cap. The Sheffield parishioners thought they would be visiting Lord Snooty; but they went away feeling sorry for the Surrey people, trapped in a life-style of uncomfortable commuting and long hours away from home.

All of it is the Church of England, and the Church is dedicated to staying in the inner cities. Spires still standing as part of landscapes changed out of recognition by demolition and rebuilding give some sense of continuity to those who have never been inside the building. They still like to know the church is there, and they are the ones it goes on seeking to serve. Canon Donald Nicholson,

when he was at St Mary's, Bourne Street, in London, used to see
the rubbish shutes on each floor of the huge council blocks labelled 'Dust and ashes' and they made him think, 'Exult, O dust and
ashes, The Lord shall be thy part . . .' One day; perhaps not yet.

CHAPTER FIVE

Social Joys

Church furnishing! church furnishing!
Sing art and crafty praise!
He gave the brass for burnishing
He gave the thick red baize.
                              (*John Betjeman*)

CHURCH OF ENGLAND PEOPLE are such nice people, with nice manners, so why do they have so many rows – over the furniture, the organ, the reordering, the PCC elections...? Why are clergy persistently driven ragged by in-fighting in the parish?

'Oh, I'm all right, really; just exhausted,' says one priest at the end of his tether, who could be any of them out there in the Church of England heartlands. He has a thriving parish in church-going country, and the people are 'lovely'. As a popular hymn puts it, 'what social joys are there'. But to preserve him from too much job satisfaction, there is a small clique of articulate Anglicans whose mission is to oppose and challenge the vicar at every turn, and from time to time, to use their undoubted know-how to invoke the Church's legal system. There are lots of people in various places would think this was about them.

Probably the rest are too nice to take them on. Niceness could yet be the undoing of the C of E. It reaches a peak in middle-church, middle-class parishes, where being nice is often felt to be the basis of true religion, though it does break down at some points. The great Church of England middle hates and distrusts 'extremes', and sees no cause to be nice to those who hold unpopular or politically incorrect convictions, especially if it suspects that they are not being terribly nice about it.

The bishops are nice, too, which may be why they maintain a

united front literally at all costs – collegiality or bust. 'Our leaders are tremendously anxious to avoid controversy, therefore things go untackled and fester too long,' says a senior priest responsible for a huge heap of masonry and the human beings who live in its parish. 'I want to grasp a nettle or lance a boil right away. I often surprise parishioners. I turn up on the doorstep and say, "I hear you're not happy with me. Tell me about it." Then I can say, "I care, too, from a different angle from yours, so let's work from there." A lot more robustness is needed at the top. The leaders of the Church think that if they ignore a problem it will go away, but you want to lance the boil and pour on the iodine. It will hurt like hell, but it will heal the quicker. Parish priests know that, but the bishops are not parish priests, and they don't know.'

The heartlands of the Church of England may be in different places for different people, but in terms of numbers, strength and intense activity they are in the suburbs outside cities, and in small towns with big churches. As an epitome of suburbia there is Wimbledon, an upmarket part of the diocese of Southwark, a magical name for millions of tennis buffs, a reminder of summer and strawberries even for the uncommitted. For the people of St Mary's Church the tennis is 'a regular annual commitment for a bonanza fortnight', says Canon Gerald Parrott, speaking at the end of seven years as Team Rector of Wimbledon. Since they went in for running a car park and doing teas, the fortnight brings in about £10,000. 'We have a field right next door to the church, rather like a village green. People are desperate for every inch of ground during Wimbledon, and we used to let it out as just a car park, but now we do home-made, picknicky things, and it draws in people outside the church to help. It's the X and Y principle. If you set up project X, what matters is that the result is Y. It's a justifiable exercise in itself, but the spin-off benefits are more important.'

They give the money away to national, overseas and local charities, and: 'It's also a way in which we assist the finances of other parishes. We're one of five parishes in this diocese with huge quotas that help to maintain poorer churches – we pay £110,000

– so we say unashamedly on the paper that we support the Church in inner-city south London. But the leading lay people say they can see real difficulties if the quota goes up any more, and they are very angry about the Church Commissioners' misdeeds, especially as we have senior accountant types here who thought they showed extraordinary incompetence.

'We get between thirty-five and forty to a said communion at eight on Sundays, and about 140 communicants to a sung eucharist at half-past-nine, and it would double the number if all who come came every week. Thirty come to matins, and twenty-five or thirty to sung evensong, but the Sunday School is the most significant thing that has happened. There would be three hundred if they all came. They come in from the hall for the blessing and fill the chancel with a minimum amount of disruption. The last hymn is always a children's hymn. Parents respond to a provision they think is jolly good for their children, we see young dads carrying the babies up the aisle, and it's a huge sort of conformity thing; they want to do what the others do. Our name is known, and we don't need to ask. It reflects the fact that parts like this will still respond to what the Church of England offers if it's doing it jolly well.'

St Mary's has the problem now common to the outer parishes: how to deepen the commitment of the new influx. Canon Parrott doubts the wisdom of sweeping priests away from the Church's areas of strength. 'Mervyn Stockwood had a slogan: "Reinforce success". If you're making inroads, don't sabotage it by having anything other than proper staffing and all that. Mind you spread the manure evenly over the ground. More doors open here than in the inner-city, and there could well be a rethinking about this. Where the Church has success reinforce it, don't weaken it. Because of church planting, because of Evangelicals in particular, and because we are neither "Catholic" nor Evangelical, we draw people with strong leanings towards the centre. It proves that if someone is prepared to work jolly hard in a place like this, the best of non-extreme Anglicanism will really work.'

The Revd Mavis Wilson, who is married to the Vicar of Christ

Church, Epsom Common, is adviser in mission and evangelism for the diocese of Guildford, the kind of area which used to be known as gin and Jaguar country, and is still what P. G. Wodehouse would describe as 'oofy'. 'It's full of people who commute to London, stuffed with people who have high-power jobs,' she says. 'They are well-informed, very competent, and short of time, and I should think that in our 162 parishes we probably have a higher proportion of gifted people than anywhere in the country.

'Money has not been a problem here, though that is changing, and there is a lot of discussion on how the Church can be financed through a system which encourages parishes to take responsibility. There is a certain amount of realistic understanding that it was not real money that the Church Commissioners lost, but there are those who understand over-commitment, and they do hold the Commissioners to be realistically responsible, though this diocese is affected less than most. Clergy pensions are a bigger concern.'

Evangelism takes money, too. 'Young families are coming in because the local churches are working much harder with the realities of the situation, which is that people have not the basics of the faith. But we have to work harder still, over baptisms, to help them move, and with children; and work with children is the most difficult. It's difficult to get people to volunteer, especially for youth work, so more parishes are working towards employing paid youth workers, and it's having an effect. At Epsom Common we have a church plant on an estate, and an open youth group with a youth worker responsible for it. In Guildford diocese the move is towards paid employees and administrators, which does reflect a level of affluence. But people have to be persuaded to produce money, and they will if they can see clearly what it's for, and I suspect that must be true in the wider Church of England. People know that administrators free the incumbent for other things and get him away from his computer.'

Mrs Wilson was working on plans for the diocesan initiative in evangelism in 1996, from Lent to Pentecost: 'The Pilgrims' Way', which took its name from the old pilgrimage routes across the diocese from Winchester to Canterbury. It was to be 'a reminder that all Christians are on a journey ... and that evangelism is about helping others to take a step forwards towards faith in Christ'. A tall order?

They had to look at their buildings, thinking of ways to make the church more user-friendly and the worship more 'open, accessible, varied and alive'. To those who understand the language the choice of words carries the message that not all the faithful in the diocese of Guildford were going to enthuse about this, for it seems to be about reordering, about worship songs, a touch of the happy-clappy; and tradition gets in the way.

'The problem,' Mavis Wilson says, 'is people who don't want to change things. A variety of worship styles are required, quite a lot of family services, and looking at the church's relevance to newcomers, which is something established congregations aren't always ready to do, but they've got to be. We have a commitment to adult initiation, and that's why the Alpha course has taken off so well here: a three-months-long weekly course which combines group experience, fellowship, teaching and discussion. We're enormously bad at saying to people, "Do you turn to Christ?" We're always ready to think the best of people, but we don't actually ask. Alpha isn't the only model, there's the catechumenate, and we're working with an aim – though we shan't achieve it – that by the year 2000 every parish in the diocese will have an adult initiation process. I don't mean a confirmation group, because we're taking people from wherever they are; they are on a process of exploration, and if at the end they say "No", we respect that. It's an answer of integrity.

'Look at people under the age of forty: most have had no Sunday School and no Christian teaching at all; so we must go further back than just asking, "Do you want to be confirmed?" Church people are so nice, so polite, and so reserved: reserved about their faith, so it's difficult for them to talk about it. We have to encourage them to put it into words, and tell them, "Understand that what you say is just a little bit in a person's journey". I don't think people are as hostile to the faith as they were twenty years ago. The climate is different now. It's interesting.'

The Church is also booming in the suburbs of the northern cities, where – as in London – the beleaguered parishes of the inner city know that a mile or two up the road there is an entirely different scenario. The Revd Godfrey Butland went to Allerton, in outer Liverpool, after thirteen years in Everton. 'This is a part of Liverpool where people still go to church. We come from an inner-city parish, and we were amazed when we saw the people coming in,' says his wife, Lesley.

Godfrey Butland finds Allerton is typical of the difference between inner cities and suburbia. 'I sometimes rationalise it by thinking of pluses and minuses. In suburbia there are many more people to share the responsibilities and keep the show on the road, but in suburbia you get a much bigger fringe. Those who came at Everton were convinced of their faith, and made great sacrifices for it. Here there is a committed corps, but a larger corps who come every few weeks, and I'm learning to be more cautious about my use of the word "commitment", which has been part of my vocabulary, because to talk about it makes another stress factor.'

He has been told that if he were to talk of tithing, people would become defensive. 'I think I'll heed that warning, but talk about something like "first fruits". People are tied up in all sorts of ways, and their giving to God is low down. They need to think about their ordering of giving: do they give to God what's left over, or the first fruits of what they bring home? I was reading through the representations the PCC formed when they were looking for a new incumbent, and one thing was that we give away one tenth of our church income. That turned out to be one tenth of what was left; and that may be how people think of their personal giving.

'We have lots of professional people, teachers, retired, a few accountants, mostly middle management. In terms of diocesan quota we're ninth out of 204 – £35,000 rising to £40,000. There'll be eight parishes asked to find an extra 20 per cent, and by 1997 half our income will be going on quota. We have quota by the potential system, the inner city pay less and we pay considerably more, and coming from the inner city I can see the benefits from the other end. But when you reach half your income . . . there are some rumblings that questions should be asked, though most take the view that it has happened and there's no point in moaning.

'I've found some very hungry people here. My predecessor did a great job at clearing away the rock and stone, and he thought the time had come for planting. He and his colleague told me of a real eagerness to move in the area of faith. He had enormous problems, for example, trying to wean the parish off matins. Once they had temporary scaffolding up in church, for the new lighting, and one man who always sat in his own seat still insisted on sitting there, so he climbed inside the scaffolding – and couldn't get out. But when he discovered that matins had gone, he left the church.

'I'd say our priority was taking people along a spiritual journey of faith, and finding so many people who want to move. I'm encouraging people to be more honest with each other in terms of expressing their faith, and it's hard for some who say they always thought the Christian faith was a private matter between them and God. It's difficult for them.

'My heart goes out to people, sometimes, they have so many pressures on them, bearing their own burdens. One Wednesday morning at the mid-week communion a lady in her eighties was there who doesn't usually come, very composed and dignified, and as she left she said, "My brother has died." Later I went round to see how she was, and she said, "I'm so sorry to have burdened you, you must have so many things to think about." I said, "What do you think I'm here for?" and she replied, "My mother always told me never to make a fuss." I want to encourage people to talk more.'

The Revd Dr John Fenwick left the Archbishop of Canterbury's staff at Lambeth in 1992 to go north to the commuter parish of St Laurence's, Chorley, in Lancashire, where people who live in houses which were built in the 1970s travel daily to Preston, Blackburn, Manchester and Liverpool. Once there were forty cotton mills in the neighbourhood; then Chorley was to be a new town, but it never happened though the plan did give rise to some estates. 'It's a mixture. Some people had their ancestors here, others moved in last year,' Dr Fenwick says.

He has not had an easy ride. There were times when Lambeth would have seemed tranquillity itself by comparison, for St Laurence's made headlines during 1995, when a breakaway group of eighteen people on the parochial church council set up an alternative PCC. There was a long wrangle over the date of the annual parochial meeting. The group invoked the Church Representation Rules and threatened to take court proceedings against the Bishop of Blackburn when he intervened on behalf of the rector and the rest of the congregation. The eighteen formed the Parishioners' Society on a nationwide basis, offering to advise other lay people about their rights, and the row continued on various fronts. But through it all, the parish grew and flourished: 150 on a normal Sunday, between 200 and 250 at the family service on parade Sunday.

New young families come in, bringing the parish the same challenge facing other churches outside cities. 'Part of the problem is that people come with a lot of goodwill because it's good for their children, and the parental knowledge of the faith is quite hazy. The challenge is to turn that into a more informed faith in a way that doesn't frighten them away in the first fortnight.

'But we're growing into it. We try to be user-friendly at baptisms, with a knock-on effect. We lay what it's all about before the families in a fairly up-front way, and the final decision about whether to go ahead lies with them. We visit with an anniversary card up to the age of five, so that they feel the church is welcoming and friendly, then if they have a second child you get another bite of the cherry. It's useful that we have a school, and I have children there myself, so I'm there at the gates, smiling away. Parents of children I baptised are now applying to join the school.

'There's an increasing thirst for knowledge, people are asking for courses. I remember that John Finney said in his book *Finding Faith Today* that it takes four years for someone to come to faith – not that if it hasn't happened in six months it's a failure. We've adopted the Bishop of Blackburn's mission statement, that we are Christ's ambassadors, and we've set ourselves the vision to be a worshipping, caring, outreaching, serving community.

'We have six lay assistants licensed to administer communion in people's houses and old people's homes, and we've sent a second person to train as a Reader. I find it encouraging that we're getting donations for young people's work, like the £400 that came from the family of an old parishioner who died. Ten years ago that would have been for the roof fund. Someone said to my wife early on, when we began to get young people coming to church, "It's made coming to church all these years worthwhile, just to know that it will go on after I'm dead." '

Canon Terry Grigg, a former General Synod member, is no stranger to strife at St Mary's, Cottingham, in the suburbs of Hull. A row over a statue of the Virgin Mary (described at the consistory court as 'Italianate', which it certainly was) ran and ran in the media. Most of the congregation liked the statue and wanted to keep it, but one group succeeded in getting it banned because they argued that it was neither Anglican nor artistic. The whole to-do seems to have been a reflection of conflicts at a deeper level, for here, too, there has been more than one row surrounding the elections at the annual parochial meeting. But it all passes over the head of the populace, and St Mary's continues to draw people in.

'Some suburbs go Charismatic, we thrive on very traditional Church of England stuff,' says Canon Grigg. 'The average number at the daily mass is twenty, which is more than York Minister, and we get 200 communicants on a Sunday. There's a strong thing about parish communion, it gets people in, then they vote for people they know, and the PCC is 100 per cent *ASB* [*Alternative Service Book*]. It means the traditionalists get overlooked. I said, "Right, we'll cater for the others." So we have the Prayer Book at eight, a regular midday communion, and also a sung matins with the men and boys' choir, which is the weakest of the services, but it totters on, and I'll do it as long as people want it. After all, I say matins every day, so I might as well have them sing it with me.

'We get about seventy to evensong. I call the banns then, and we have the wedding rehearsals for the next Saturday, and once a quarter there are evening baptisms. It's a way of using the building and making sure the occasional people are helping us instead of hindering. On Whit Sunday we went outside for cakes and wine and balloons, and I preached standing on a garden seat. It's symbolic, going out preaching, like Peter. I want to make sure we're visible.'

The Church of England always appears to be flourishing in a small old town with a big church which is built into the heart of the place. The church is like a strong-box, storing centuries of significant moments in lives which may have been important only to God: but the fabric remembers them. Newark-on-Trent, in Nottinghamshire, where the spire of St Mary Magdalene's is a landmark as the inter-city trains tear through on the way to the north, is a town like that. The spire bears traces of roundhead onslaughts; Newark was a royalist stronghold in the Civil War, and this is real middle-England, where the parish church, which seats 800, is always full on Remembrance Sunday.

Plough Sunday (for the National Farmers' Union), Mothering Sunday, Harvest Festival, civic services, Chamber of Commerce, an enormous Christingle for the three schools which are historically linked with the church: nearly everyone sees the inside of the building on some special day, though most of them do not appear in between times. 'We haven't filled in the gaps, yet they would fiercely say that it's their church. Perhaps people do that in their relationships with God, slip in and out; but that he is there for them is the crucial thing,' says the Team Rector, the Revd Roger Hill. 'We're working on that. There is a sense of goodwill towards the church, and its part in the community is taken for granted. It's important that we don't take it for granted, and keep on our mettle. There's a lot of residual feeling, but the problem is that it doesn't carry on to the young people as automatically as it used to.

'Our dilemma is that the church is in the centre, a bit away from our residential community, so it's harder for them to relate to us as their parish church. As a team we're serving 26,000 people in four churches, and to be realistic, we are trying to overcome a lot of history, because going back to the last century they are all breakaways from the parish church – and it's remembered. We're trying to spell out that the team offers things individual churches wouldn't be able to do themselves. It's a balance, so that the team is not a threat but a partnership. Numbers aren't large, and with pressures on quotas, congregations have to be tested and tried. It's a very pressurised time for congregations to live in, but there is a greater partnership between clergy and lay people.'

Newark is a stop on the tourist trail; 3500 people a year sign the visitors' book, and Roger Hill thinks that this suggests a total of about 15,800 passing through, so they have taken out some pews to make a welcome area. Lay people act as guides and stewards, look after the fabric and run the coffee bar on Wednesdays and Saturdays. 'We are trying to get the building used more and more,' the rector says, and there is often an exhibition *in situ*, anything from public relations exercises by the police and the fire service to a display of patchwork; 'and the Mothers' Union did a big thing on the family'. While MU membership is falling off in some places, in Newark the Mothers' Union is growing.

On ordinary Sundays the church sees 15 to 20 people at eight, 75 to 95, including children, at parish communion (Rite A), and 15 to 20 at a Prayer Book choral evensong. People travel into Newark for the music. The parish church had a pre-Reformation Song School and the endowment from it still exists, which is why the professional director of music who presides over the all-male choir is still called the Master of the Song School. 'It's quite hard to recruit boys, and that poses the long-term question about whether to have a girls' choir. When the Master goes into the schools to ask if he can hear the boys sing, they say to him, "What about the girls?" We don't yet know where this will lead us.'

The same interesting uncertainty hangs over a number of issues. Churches in the suburbs and the small towns have the feeling that the only way left is up: and that is the path they are taking.

CHAPTER SIX

In and Out of the Closet

We, the lesbians and gay men in the pew, do more to influence the course of the Church than ten Tatchells could. We do our praying, and our work for God and the Church, while being ourselves . . . Where outing will fail, our witness will prevail. (An editorial in LGCM News, *the journal of the Lesbian and Gay Christian Movement)*

WHAT HE MISSES MOST is preaching, but it seems unlikely that he will ever stand in a pulpit again, because his speech is laboured now and not very clear, though the Scottish accent still comes through. After thirty years of ministry Fr Brian had a stroke, a bad one, and he says it was due to stress: 'The stress of being in the closet.' He was a Team Rector in the East End of London before he went to an incumbency in the north, then he had to retire at least ten years too soon because of his disabilities; but in some ways life opened up for him then. There is no more need for pretence. 'Now it's all accepted without any bother. The contrast between the secular environment and the Church is amazing.' He can be himself at last; and an important part of himself is that he is gay.

'I once remember being questioned by a bishop,' he says, 'but he wouldn't ask directly. It's a case of "You know that I know and I know you know that I know". Bishops are hung up on sexuality, but it's basically about two human beings giving each other their affection. The bishop disagreed with the homosexual life-style. I don't suppose he knows anything about it. What people are looking for in this lonely world is love.

'The bishops are all frightened, about money, mostly, and therefore about anything that might upset lay people. It's financial blackmail. Then there are the fundamentalists, trying to pretend that God wrote the Bible. If the European legislation on equality applied to the Church, the Church wouldn't get away with it.' Unsurprisingly, he does not recommend life in the closet as the way ahead for younger priests.

He is a supporter of the Aglo campaign – action for gay and lesbian ordination – because would-be ordinands are in a particularly difficult situation if they cannot come to terms with living a lie for the next forty years or so. The only way a non-celibate homosexual with a partner can get through the selection process and be ordained is to shut up like a clam, or, if asked directly, make a flat denial. Aglo, like the other homosexual pressure groups, accuses the Church of dishonesty and hypocrisy, especially since the House of Bishops spelt out its mind in a statement called *Issues in Human Sexuality*, which was published at the end of 1991. The section on The Homophile in the Life and Fellowship of the Church clearly unfolds a double standard.

Abstinence for all is presented as the ideal, but: 'At the same time there are others who are conscientiously convinced that this way of abstinence is not the best for them, and that they have more hope of growing in love for God and neighbour with the help of a loving and faithful homophile partnership, in intention lifelong, where mutual self-giving includes the physical expression of their attachment.' To them, as to all who seek to live their lives in Christ, every congregation owes friendship and understanding, the statement says. The bishops are talking about lay people here. Then, however: 'We come now to the question of the homophile clergy.' And the scene changes.

'People not only in the Church but outside it believe rightly that in the way of life of an ordained minister they ought to be able to see a pattern which the Church commends . . . This means that certain possibilities are not open to the clergy by comparison with the laity, something that in principle has always been accepted . . . We have therefore to say that in our considered judgement the clergy cannot claim the liberty to enter into sexually active homophile relationships.'

What about those in active relationships who come out as a matter of personal integrity? 'They believe their relationship to be right in the sight of God and find concealment both repugnant and destructive,' the bishops acknowledge. 'We respect that integrity.' Nevertheless: '. . . though the Church is not infallible, there is at any given time such a thing as the mind of the Church on matters of faith and life. Those who disagree with that mind are free to argue for change. What they are not free to do is to go against that mind in their own practice.'

Tim Robertson, a co-ordinator of Aglo, feels his calling is to be ordained. 'My spiritual director said from day two that I ought to go forward. The bishops have said it's all right to be gay if you keep quiet, but it's part of my identity, and I'm not prepared to let them ordain the bits they want to ordain. I understand people who make a decision not to say. Some choose to compromise; some say, "I'll come out when I'm ordained," but they go to their first job, and then their second, and in their forties or fifties they realise they've led these terribly closeted lives. I decided not to fudge it.'

Philip Groom, an Aglo supporter who works at the National Theatre and paints for the rest of the time, is a churchwarden and lay Reader at St Botolph's, Aldgate, and when he offered for ordination he had lived with his partner for fifteen years. 'How could I pretend he didn't exist? I had a series of talks with the diocesan director of ordinands and the director of women ordinands, and they decided to present me as an openly gay candidate. I was not sponsored for an Advisory Board of Ministry conference, but it was made clear to me that if I kept my mouth shut or prevaricated I'd stand a good chance. The choice was, ditch your partner, and we'll ordain you. I know priests who call their partner their lodger, or their housekeeper. It cripples your ministry; you start your ministry with one hand tied behind your back.

'The Bishop was understanding, but he could not ordain an actively gay person. Yet it's absolutely necessary for people in the front line to go forward and be shot down, for the sake of the people coming up.'

The Church has been talking round the issue for years. In 1979 a working party chaired by the then Bishop of Gloucester, the Rt Revd John Yates, completed the Gloucester report, *Homosexual Relationships*, amid a good deal of nervousness and secrecy, and it was not until 1981 that it went to the General Synod for debate. Views were diverse, to say the least, and it was agreed to take note of the report rather than recommend it for further study.

The next move came in 1987, from the Revd Tony Higton, Rector of Hawkwell, in Essex, founder of Action for Biblical Witness to Our Nation, who has won himself a high degree of unpopularity among liberals, Anglo-Catholics, even a good many of his fellow-Evangelicals, on account of his Bible-thumping denunciations of sin.

Like some others in the Church who go to extremes he is courteous and gently spoken when you meet him, unobtrusive and friendly when he is there in the flesh; but his fundamentalist interpretation of the scriptures sets people's teeth on edge, and his unsolicited mailings to brother-clergy have a knack of making them speechless with fury. Nevertheless, 167 General Synod members signed his private member's motion, which put it high enough on the list to make it the subject of another gay debate.

The Higton motion was aimed at affirming that sexual intercourse should take place only between men and women within marriage; that fornication, adultery and homosexual acts were always sinful; and that Christian leaders should set an example in sexual morality as in all spheres of morality, as a condition of being appointed to or remaining in office. The Revd Malcolm Johnson, who was then the Rector of St Botolph's, Aldgate, tried a wrecking amendment which put across a biblical interpretation of a different kind, seeing human love and its commitment to relationships as a reflection of divine love. It called for education to alert young people and parents to the dangers of promiscuity, whether it was heterosexual or homosexual, and for counsel and absolution for any who were troubled by guilt or sin 'in any aspect of their human relationships'.

It failed, as did the main motion, which was replaced by a carefully worded amendment from Bishop Michael Baughen of

Chester, so that, in the end, the Synod affirmed traditional teaching on marriage, and agreed that homosexual genital acts, like adultery and fornication – sins to be met with repentance and compassion – also 'fell short of this ideal'.

The cost of that debate in emotional terms did not emerge, but it was shattering to homosexual priests who were watching. 'I was deeply upset,' says a parish priest in the south of England, who has lived in a faithful partnership for over twenty years, though he is only in his early forties now. He fell in love with his partner at twenty-one, before he went to theological college, and nothing on the thorny path he has had to follow has changed that. The debate was one of the factors that plunged him into a long period of depression. 'I really hit the depths,' he says.

At theological college, there was a member of staff who came out about his sexuality, an act which may have cleared the way for David (which is not his real name). When the time came to leave, the college principal wanted to place him in a diocese on the other side of the country, which presented him with an impossibly difficult choice.

'My partner was working in this area, where we are now, and I had already been away for some years at college. I realised I had to say why I wouldn't go, and the principal took it quite well, really. He commended me for my honesty – I suppose he couldn't do any other after one of his staff had come out – though he said he couldn't guarantee that I would find a job where I wanted to go. But the then bishop of this diocese did come up with something. "I know where I could send you," he said. And I went to a vicar who became a very dear friend and mentor. "Have you got a girl friend?" he asked when I went for the interview. "A boy friend, then?" It would be all right, he said when I told him the truth about my homosexuality, which of course he knew anyway. "I've got one of those here already," he said.

'When I came to these parishes I very much wanted to be open with the churchwardens, but I was advised otherwise. Well, I have come out now, but only to a certain degree. While I was still very depressed I went to a confirmation in the cathedral, and I think the Spirit must have followed me home, because it came to me that I had to let my people know that I was gay. My partner said, "Do you think you should?" But I found myself telling them, and the reaction was interesting.

'Some people said they admired my courage, others thought they hadn't heard right, and asked me to repeat it. A few said quite frankly that although I was the right priest for these parishes, I should not be here, and some left, but that was balanced later by new people who came, because of course it eventually got to the local press. (They wanted me to do an interview, so I consulted with the churchwardens, who advised against it, though they said they would support me in what I decided to do, and after thinking it over I went back to them and told them I was going to talk to the reporter, which I did.) The Bishop was supportive; he had a statement prepared. But I couldn't be open about my partner, he couldn't have supported me in that – which is what I mean when I say I have come out to some degree.

'Only one man in the parish conducted a sort of campaign against me, and we managed to hold on to him until he left over something else. If people ask, "Are you a practising homosexual?" I refuse to answer. I was never very assertive before, but since I came out I have become much more so. What I do wonder sometimes is whether I shall ever be able to move. Perhaps the climate is changing; I don't know. Obviously this is going to be an issue in the present General Synod, but there are those there whose minds will remain made up whatever arguments are put to them.'

When you ask him if his partnership has been blessed he laughs and says, 'It's a bit late now, isn't it? I did do a blessing for a couple once, but it was in their house, and I'd feel a bit uneasy about doing it in church. I know one priest who conducted a blessing in church, but did so with the doors locked. When gay couples come to me I suggest they go and talk to their own parish priest. I say, "If you're rejected in your own parish, come back," and as they haven't come back, I assume it was all right.'

David shows real anxiety when he asks, 'Do people think that all homosexual priests are opposed to the ordination of women to the priesthood?' He himself affirms the ministry of women. In fact, homosexual priests are as divided on the issue as anyone else. The Lesbian and Gay Christian Movement (LGCM) is strongly pro-women, on the grounds that women, like gays, suffer from discrimination. Other gays, like some of the Anglo-Catholics in the traditionally Anglo-Catholic diocese of London, are opposed to women priests for theological or ecumenical reasons, or because they do not believe the General Synod has the authority to make a unilateral decision: and they are labelled misogynists.

In 1988 the Lambeth Conference of bishops from every part of the Anglican Communion worldwide passed a resolution which endorsed full human rights for those of 'homosexual orientation'. Two years before that the bishops of the Church of England had commissioned another report on homosexuality, which they then decided not to publish, and it was February 1990 before it leaked to the media. This was the Osborne report, by a working party of seven chaired by the Revd June Osborne, which had protected itself from 'the worst pressures of public attention' by deciding not to invite any evidence from outside bodies.

According to the Lesbian and Gay Christian Movement, the bishops disallowed publication because: 'First, they felt the report to be deficient in certain important respects, and, second, they wanted to go further towards trying to answer some of the questions it raises before making any public statement.' The statement that followed was *Issues in Human Sexuality.*

The non-publication of the Osborne report caused LGCM to launch a plan of action, pressing the Church 'to view lesbian and gay sexuality and heterosexuality as equally valid'. The movement endorsed the Osborne report's recommendation that 'further study and research should be taken on unresolved questions about homosexuality', but it had criticisms on a number of points, including the 'neutral' description of various counselling groups. LGCM is still angry about the damage it believes is done by Evangelical groups which take the line that gay people can be changed into straight people, and it found that the Osborne report made no

distinction between them and the counselling groups which hold
a positive view about gay and lesbian sexuality.

There are gay Evangelicals, but they keep a low profile, which
allows many Evangelicals to believe that the problem does not
exist in their churches. A non-academic survey carried out mainly
among members of LGCM's Evangelical Fellowship had fifty-eight
men and twelve women declaring that their churches would expect
them to undergo some form of deliverance or healing if they were
found out. One man out of the eighty male respondents (of whom
the largest group were Anglican) had moved from homosexuality
to heterosexuality and eight others said they hoped such a change
would happen for them: a hope unlikely to be expressed by gays
on the Catholic wing.

LGCM was celebrating its twentieth birthday in 1996. The Revd
Richard Kirker, its secretary since 1979, was ordained deacon by
Lord Runcie, who was Bishop of St Albans at the time, but he
never made any secret of his homosexuality, and he has not been
priested. His office is in Oxford House, at Bethnal Green in east
London, where towards the end of the last century young gentlemen from Oxford University used to set aside their privileged life-
style to live and work among the poor. It is an impressive red
brick building, worthy of Keble College, where the plans were
made for an Anglican Church settlement which would show pro-
spective clergymen the problems of city poverty at first hand.

Oxford House, with its waft of lunchtime curry hanging about
the entrance, is still a base for community work in Bethnal Green,
for although the place has grown more prosperous there are plenty
of tensions and needs. It was a Tractarian foundation, an
expression of the social conscience which grew out of the Oxford
Movement. Richard Kirker is inclined to think that with the presence there of LGCM, things have come full circle, for the majority
of gay priests come from the Church's Catholic wing, and like the
old Anglo-Catholic priests of the East End they labour devotedly
in their parishes, and kindle flames of faith where fires are not
easily lit.

In spite of assurances in the bishops' statement, Richard Kirker maintains that candidates are asked about their sexuality, and that the Church is not supportive. 'It picks an argument with them from the start. Some selectors, when they are assessing maturity and psychological well-being, often take it upon themselves to find out if he's in a relationship. The question is asked sometimes directly, sometimes obliquely.

'Time and time we hear from diocesan directors of ordinands not to answer honestly. There are cases where bishops have said that once a candidate is recommended for training, and takes the bishop into his confidence, the bishop has to say, "Don't tell anyone. Deny it if you're asked."

'On the day the report came out one bishop rang about forty priests he knew, and said, "I want you to know that we in this diocese are going to take no notice of *Issues in Human Sexuality*. You have as much support from your bishops today as you had yesterday." To do anything else would have been to add isolation to the sense of being kicked in the teeth.'

LGCM keeps an open list in its newsletters for those who want to publish their names, but it has never outed anyone. It is the secular pressure group, Outrage, which uses shock tactics to fight the homophobia it claims to see in the Church. Its leader, Peter Tatchell, and his troops have erupted into Church meetings as if they were the SAS, and broken up press briefings in Church House, Westminster, with shouts of 'Stop Crucifying Gays' and ear-piercing whistle blasts that drive everyone out of the room.

When the General Synod met at Church House on 30 November 1994 Outrage were out the front steps 'outing' ten bishops whose names were displayed on their banners, but it was a hit-or-miss kind of list, unsupported by any sort of proof. It did, however, give impetus to serious talks between senior churchmen and members of gay and lesbian organisations, which began about two weeks later. But the real drama was still to come.

On Monday morning, 13 March 1995, Dr David Hope, who was then Bishop of London, summoned members of the media to London House to hear his public response to implied threats in a letter from Peter Tatchell which the Bishop's lawyers regarded as 'intimidatory or worse'. Mr Tatchell had asked for an interview the previous January, and after a wide-ranging conversation which lasted for about forty minutes he handed the Bishop a letter in a sealed envelope.

The letter said: 'Although Outrage has been passed a lot of detailed information about your personal life which would have enabled us to confidently name you at Synod on 30 November, we chose not to do so. The reason is this: we believe that you are, or can be, a person of honesty and courage. You have the potential to play a very special role, both morally and historically. It is our sincere hope that you will find the inner strength and conviction to realise the importance of voluntarily coming out as gay, and of speaking in defence of lesbian and gay rights.'

The letter went on to suggest that if Dr Hope was concerned about acting alone, a number of bishops might make a joint declaration of their gay orientation. 'That way you could give each other support and solidarity, and protect yourselves against being picked off one by one.'

The Bishop spelt out his own position with clarity and courage. 'I have from the beginning chosen to lead a single, celibate life. This is a positive way for me. I am happy and content with and within myself. I enjoy the company of both men and women.' Answering questions, he said: 'I'm trying to be as open and honest as I can here. I am leading a celibate life and I am content with myself. I'm not a sexually active person. Some people are quite clear that they are homosexual, or that they are heterosexual; others are less sure. There is a certain ambiguity about it. I think that is where I stand. I still take the view that sexual acts are for within marriage. Outside of marriage I still feel those are not acceptable.'

It was a brilliant parrying stroke, a bold gamble; and it came off. Peter Tatchell was rent asunder by every newspaper from *The Times* to *The Sun*. The Primates of the Anglican Communion, who were meeting at Windsor, sent Dr Hope a message of solidarity 'in deploring this reprehensible intrusion into your private life', and conveyed their 'deepest affection and prayerful support'. Lord

Templeman, chairman of the Ecclesiastical Committee in Parliament, was 'appalled at the accusation that the Bishop of London is gay', and said: 'The insinuation that he has ever indulged in anything that the Church would regard as immoral is quite outrageous to anyone who knows him.'

Shortly afterwards, the Bishop of Southwark, the Rt Revd Roy Williamson, who comes from the Evangelical wing, went so far as to say in a BBC Radio 4 interview that he would consider ordaining a practising homosexual in an open relationship. When the question was put to him he replied: 'That entirely depends on whether that relationship may be stable or not . . . I simply don't interfere in that kind of thing.' He was jumped on by Evangelicals in his diocese, by leading members of the conservative Evangelical group, Reform, and by Evangelical brother-bishops.

Next day he produced a statement of elucidation, explaining that his comment was an honest, if impromptu answer to an honest question. 'It reflects the genuine struggle within myself to relate tradition and experience. It needs to be taken in the context of my desire to uphold the current teaching of the Church and, at the same time, to exercise a sensitive pastoral ministry.' He acknowledged the importance of the House of Bishops statement, with its denial of gay sexual relationships for the clergy; but he said the essence of his own pastoral struggle, which was shared by many others, was also a legitimate contribution.

The *Church Times* commented on the stirring events of the previous few days: 'Dr Hope writes of being constantly under "well nigh impossible pressure" from lobbies on both sides of the argument. This week he wrested that argument from the bullies. His reward should be some indication that the Church can tackle the issue of sexuality calmly and openly, without prurience, without sensation, but with dignity and love.' A month later, on the Tuesday of Holy Week, it was announced that David Hope would be the next Archbishop of York.

Richard Kirker remains bitter about what happened to Bishop Roy Williamson. 'He was picked off. That humiliating retraction . . . What shocked was that the Evangelicals, his natural constituency, reacted in such an unpleasant way and that those who agreed with him offered no support. The trouble was that the bishops who do ordain have not formed into an identifiable caucus. They could do as those in support of women priests did, and declare themselves. They definitely will have ordained – but will they say they have?'

Peter Tatchell has defended the tactics of Outrage. 'Our deliberately shocking and provocative style aims to grab media attention (lobbying MPs and writing letters rarely gets on the news bulletins). Press and broadcasting coverage is vital to communicate the lesbian and gay agenda to the wider public and to generate a momentum for social change. Without media coverage, queer issues remain invisible, and there is no pressure for reform.'

Lesbian and gay people are split over their views on the way Outrage goes to work. *Gay Times* said the letter to Dr Hope was 'a gentle, courteous and completely non-threatening request for the Bishop to come out with dignity', which many would feel it was not. The paper described the Bishop's response as 'a shrewd move from a consummate church politician', which it was.

The much-reviled Mr Tatchell has his defenders: those who feel betrayed because Church leaders they believe to be homosexual will not forge a way out of the closet for them by declaring themselves. 'Did you see what Peter Tatchell wrote to David Hope? It was a wonderful letter, full of charity and understanding,' says one priest. 'I know Peter. He wasn't to blame,' says another gay priest, a man in his early forties, who is, at the time of writing, unemployed. In the job he lost, Derek (which is not his real name) was curate at a rather 'stuffy' urban church, in a prosperous part of the town, but where a lot of people are alone and lonely. His long-standing partner, Henry (not his real name either), a professional man, and a committed Anglican, lived with him in his house, and everything seemed to be all right, until a reasonable-sounding excuse was found, and he was told it would be best if he left. Derek and Henry did not proclaim their relationship but they never tried to disguise it.

'Every Sunday we cooked lunch for parishioners. I was certainly

tolerated,' Henry says. Derek reflects, 'I don't think people necessarily clicked that Henry was my partner. The ones with a bit
more nous about them realised, but those were generally supportive anyway. Those who wouldn't have been supportive just thought
he was a frightfully nice chap sharing my house, and wasn't it
kind that he cooked Sunday lunch for them; because he always
did the cooking. It worked quite well, really.'

'That was part of his ministry, yes, a sort of theology of Sunday
lunch. I did what I could to ease the burden for him. On the
surface, the vicar and his wife tolerated me, in fact we had them
round twice,' Henry comments.

'They never invited us back, though, did they?' adds Derek.

Derek says he has always wanted to live openly. 'We feel we
were honest about our relationship. We don't pretend it doesn't
exist. I've always felt it was the only way I could live, because it
would be more stressful to try and cloak things. It's not a great
sort of moral thing that I'm out, it's more my own psychological
welfare.'

They are dismissive about the House of Bishops statement. 'It's
the Church doing what it's good at, which is hypocrisy. If they
don't want homosexuals in the clergy let them get rid of every
homosexual clergyman, and some dioceses would collapse. Then
let them deal with the outrage. Oh, yes, there would be outrage,
international outrage, if you had people witch-hunted out of their
jobs which they've been doing for twenty years or more,' Derek
says.

'It's quite cowardly, really, because they're too frightened to
offend anybody.'

'They say it's all right for the laity to have partners but not for
the clergy, and that's not the only double standard. There's the
load of clergy who are gay and the bishops know they're gay, and
they're allowed, and they get preferment as long as they keep
quiet. They should have taken it all on board before Higton, and
nipped it in the bud then. The Evangelicals have got stronger
and stronger.'

'I find it offensive,' Henry says, 'those job advertisements that specify married men with children. In no other job would people be allowed to say that. It's quite clear there are large sections of the laity who have no intention of extending a welcome to gay clergy, let alone gay couples. Well, the Evangelical churches are not going to, are they?

'We went to an ordination, and when the ordinands received communion the wives and families were invited up with them. It was like a badge of heterosexuality. It was the ordinands who were being ordained, not the families.'

What if the Church were to acknowledge stable gay relationships? 'Oh, it would make a tremendous difference,' says Derek. 'I would feel I could engage in a full and open ministry, not only giving all of myself, but Henry giving a lot of himself, as well.'

'And for the laity,' says Henry, 'if it was regularised, legitimised in terms of acceptance by the institution, then we'd be more comfortable. One of the things was that there were same-sex couples in the congregation where we were, but they tended to hang back. Well, it was that sort of place, you know . . .'

'Stuffy.'

'Stuffy, yes. Yet despite the battering we've both had we still have a love for the Anglican Church, a deep affection; we'd like to see it prosper. But we do feel we've been locked out of it.'

Derek says, 'There's no way I would want to be back in parochial ministry, no way. We'd live in fear and trembling, and we've been through that once. We don't want to go through it again. You might get a change of bishop, who would throw you out, unless you've got the freehold and aren't bothered about moving. I have friends who are vicars, and I've said to them, "Why don't you come out?" They say, "Because I want to move. I don't want to stay here for the rest of my ministry." Take away the freehold and you do expose clergy to the bigotry of churchwardens, congregations and so on.

'In my sort of way, I've been aware of my gayness from an early age, and I always felt an outsider. It's a very common experience among gay children. When I actually presented myself for a selection conference there was no way that I was going to pretend. I desperately, desperately wanted to be accepted for myself, and I felt I *was* accepted, eventually. The church was a surrogate family, and that's, again, about being accepted; but you don't want to be in a family that hates you, where the question asked is, "When are you leaving?" '

The Church's struggles with sex are not confined to the gay issue. Clergy marriages break down at the rate of one a week, according to an estimate quoted by Broken Rites, the support group for divorced and separated clergy wives. Increasing clergy stress is usually blamed, and there is also the fact that things which used to be unthinkable now pass as fairly unremarkable, even when clergymen are involved.

Two-thirds of the vicarage tragedies are brought about by the husbands' adultery, usually after the marriage has lasted many years. Most deserted wives are in their forties or a good deal older when they find themselves cast adrift. The vicarage is a tied house; there is no marital home to be sold for a sharing out of assets, and not much to expect in the way of maintenance for her and any dependent children.

'One weekend my husband decided to take his "girlfriend" to Paris,' says an associate member writing to the quarterly newsletter, *Rite Lines* (she is an associate because her marriage has miraculously survived). 'The Sunday services were covered, the suitcase half packed, and shirts washed and ironed. I was very distressed, even more so when the churchwarden came to see me. He said, "If the Vicar goes to Paris that is the end of his ministry." '

She was one of the lucky ones. 'On the Thursday evening the "girlfriend" phoned to say she couldn't go to Paris, as one of her children was ill, and her mother didn't want the responsibility of a sick child as well as two others for the weekend. We have just had our thirty-seventh wedding anniversary. My husband and I have both worked hard in our parishes, and worked well together, but caring for divorced members of our church has been a great strain on us. After the five-year relationship ended my husband met his friend again, in London, and couldn't see what he had seen in her. He thanked me for not divorcing him.'

Broken Rites was formed in 1983, largely because of action taken by Frank Field MP, an active churchman and a Member of Parliament with a particular concern for social issues. He was appalled when he discovered how often deserted and separated clergy wives were left to sink or swim, and after inviting letters from anyone affected, he wrote a report called *Passing By on the Other Side*, which set things moving.

'There is now a lot less sweeping it under the carpet,' says the secretary, Pam Dawson, who spends more and more time listening to the tales of distress which come over her telephone. One was from a young wife, deserted with four children, one under a year, one aged seven, and twins in between.

'But the big issue is pensions. A wife can work with her husband for the whole of his ministry, and then have no share in his pension. One clergy wife was sixty-three when she was divorced. He remarried and died within a month, and she gets nothing. But nothing can be done without legislation.'

Frank Field has been aware of this problem from the start. In the annual report he tells members that in 1995 the Pensions Management Institute, working with the Law Society, came up with some clear proposals about enabling all wives to claim a share of the pension. The issue is moving up the political agenda. When success comes, Broken Rites will have done a good deal to bring it about, for it was one of the first organisations to start campaigning on this particular need.

CHAPTER SEVEN

A Gospel To Proclaim

> When I saw various members of my staff rolling round
> on our blue carpet, from one end to the other, which is a
> considerable length, I went back to my study and said, 'Lord,
> is everything going to be all right?' (The Revd John Irvine,
> in the Holy Trinity, Brompton, newspaper, Focus)

STORIES ABOUT EVANGELICALS usually begin with 'More than . . .'.
'More than 70,000 will have attended Spring Harvest at its three
sites in eight different weeks.' 'More than 100,000 people will
have attended Alpha courses during 1995.' 'More than 9000 church
leaders have attended Alpha conferences since May 1993.' Non-
Evangelicals sometimes feel sour about what looks to them very
much like a numbers game.

Spring Harvest, which happens every year, is a an action-packed
Christian holiday, probably the biggest annual Christian gathering
in Europe, with a glossy brochure full of events for those 'wanting
to learn and laugh and to make friends, and to do some deep
business with God' (in the words of the Provost of Bradford, the
Very Revd John Richardson).

Alpha is a fifteen-session course for non-churchgoers and new
Christians, emanating from Holy Trinity, Brompton (HTB), in
London, and rushing through mainly Evangelical churches in many
parts of the world like the wind of the Holy Spirit, to which it is
thought to be closely related. As the Alpha mission statement puts
it: 'Thousands of churches run the Alpha course as an ongoing
programme of evangelism. Millions come to Christ, be filled with
the Spirit, and tell others about Jesus. Churches grow to capacity,
with thousands of new churches planted.' More than 1600 Alpha
courses are running in Britain – many more, no doubt, since

'dozens more are registering every month'. At HTB itself, 'more than 550 people take part in each evening Alpha course'.

They could be among those ripe to be 'slain in the Spirit', thrown to the floor laughing uncontrollably, howling, even barking under the influence of 'the Toronto Blessing', which swept across the Atlantic from the Toronto Airport Christian Fellowship to HTB in May 1994, and out from there to many other places, even rural Gloucestershire. It first hit HTB at a staff meeting, when one member arrived after paying a visit to John and Eleanor Mumford, at a Vineyard network church in south London, and everyone fell to the floor, laughing. Mrs Mumford was invited to speak, to share the experiences which came upon her and her husband in Toronto, and from then on the Spirit exploded into action with no holds barred. As the story emerged, fashionable HTB, looking sedate and ordinary at the end of its avenue of trees, was beseiged by thousands of sightseers and seekers queuing in the hope of finding a space inside, and what else it was that many of them found there – no one can exactly say.

Nine months later, the Revd Bill Heald, Vicar of St Luke's, Redcliffe Square, nearby, was telling a church leaders' gathering at HTB of a visitation in his own parish, at a meeting in the house of one of the churchwardens. The Holy Spirit alighted first on the secretary of the PCC, then came upon the others, and: 'One person seemed to have an engine inside him, because he was all over the floor and filled with power, just not able to contain it. The house was shaking . . . Just as we were leaving, I looked round the room and it looked probably worse than the aftermath of a New Year's Eve party in Scotland. The pictures were askew and the furniture was all over the place.'

People began to make pilgrimages to the Airport Church in Toronto, among them Sandy Millar, the Vicar of Holy Trinity, Brompton, and Bishop David Pytches, of St Andrew's, Chorleywood, with his wife, Mary. Mrs Pytches said afterwards that she lay on the floor, wailing, though she had hoped for laughter. 'And there was this incredible roaring. I felt that this roar was a prophetic roar, like the Lion of Judah roaring, and the children are beginning to gather. The prodigals are coming home. Something is happening.'

Whatever was happening, it made the rest of the Church distinctly uneasy. The Dean of Worcester, the Very Revd Robert Jeffery, reflected the view of most of the Church of England when he wrote his preface to the 1995 *Church of England Year Book*: 'The so-called "Toronto Blessing" now witnessed in some charismatic churches, revealed in fits of laughter and falling about during worship, is not a sign of revival. It is an expression of mass hysteria for which there is ample historical precedence. There is a danger that it will lead to a ghetto mentality and the undermining of an intellectually respectable expression of faith.'

The Dean was taken to task by Bishop Lesslie Newbigin, a theologian who has lectured at the HTB Bible School, who wrote to the *Church Times* to say that Dean Jeffrey was mistaken in his judgement. Some of the manifestations did seem odd, he admitted. 'But one has to ask two questions: is the genuine fruit of the Spirit present? and second, do those involved remain at the stage of mere emotional excitement? The answer to the first of these questions is yes, and to the second, no ... I have the feeling that one gets when the monsoon breaks after a very dry summer.'

The monsoon was tempered at the end of 1995. The Airport Church which gave its name to the Toronto Blessing was expelled from the worldwide Vineyard network, because the Vineyard leader, the Californian evangelist John Wimber, became concerned about its focus on dramatic manifestations and the interpretations put upon them. HTB, undeterred, took the break as a warning 'that we must continue to take care about what we do'.

Monsoons apart, Evangelicals have gained strength so rapidly in recent years that many people think they are in the process of taking over the Church of England, but like many questions that come up in the C of E it depends whom one asks, for Evangelicals will often say they feel marginalised by the liberal ascendency and are left defending biblical truths from a ghetto. Nothing is as simple as it looks. Neither view is too far from the mark.

Are they taking over? 'No,' says Canon Michael Saward of St

Paul's Cathedral, a member of the Church of England Evangelical
Council. 'They'll blow it again. They always have.' Michael Saward
served on the General Synod for twenty years. While he was Vicar
of Ealing from 1978 to 1991 his family had to live through the
trauma of a particularly violent attack which ended in what
the tabloids called 'the vicarage rape'. Now he lives in Amen
Court, the home of the Dean and Chapter of St Paul's: a deceptively
peaceful-looking oasis only a stone's throw from the Old Bailey,
and a quiet, green close where the traffic noises from Newgate
Street nearby hardly penetrate.

Numbers, he explains, are not the same thing as power. 'Since
the last eight years or so, some Evangelicals are performing
according to tradition. The moment they get near a position of
power they disintegrate. Somehow they don't know how to
handle power, because they assume that power means corruption.
They were torn by events in the sixteenth century, pushed by
Archbishop Laud in the seventeenth century so that practically all
of them left, and then in the eighteenth century came Wesley. After
that they grew and grew, but in the ninteenth century, just when
everything looked promising . . .

'Well, Palmerston was not much interested in the Church, so he
got Shaftesbury to find him some bishops, and Shaftesbury put up
a lot of Evangelical names.' Canon Saward goes to his bookshelves
and reads from *Christian England*, by David Edwards, volume iii,
page 172: 'The Evangelical peer [Shaftesbury] produced for him
[Palmerston] nineteen hard-working if dull pastors.' Shaftesbury
wanted Evangelical bishops, and the ones he chose, like most
Evangelical clergymen of the period, were simple and godly, as
Owen Chadwick says in the first volume of his study of *The
Victorian Church*.

Simple godliness, perhaps a desirable quality in a bishop even
now, was not enough on its own without the back-up of a harder
edge and the capacity to lead, direct and inspire. 'So in the mid-
nineteenth century, when they really had the opportunity, they
hadn't got the men for the job; and that has been the constant
problem,' the Canon reflects. 'We had fourteen Evangelicals on

the Bench. It's seriously questionable whether we can find men of the next generation to replace them.

'Where most Evangelicals are uneasy is about Charismatics, because they're very bad for any real concern about the institutional life of the Church. A large number of under-forty-fives have been influenced by Charismatics, and are not concerned with the institutional Church at all. They are good at evangelising, good on personal spirituality, but they can't cope with institutions.

'On present numbers, we ought to have two-thirds of the House of Bishops, but we shan't get it. A diocesan bishop needs to have been an archdeacon, or a suffragan, and how do they become one of those? Where there is only a single suffragan in a diocese, the diocesan never appoints an Evangelical. Where there is a team you might get two or three Evangelical suffragans, but we are much lower in suffragans than diocesans, and the same is true of archdeacons. It's harder for a youngish man to get appointed if he's an Evangelical, because the liberal Catholics have merrily appointed their own clones. Anglo-Catholics sometimes do, but Evangelical bishops are less willing to appoint their own for fear of being partisan. Other traditions would have made some to keep the tradition going.

'Young middle-aged men must be blooded; and if you have a growing number of Evangelicals in the Church it is perfectly logical to have a growing number of appointments, but few Evangelicals have a national perspective. So if you are an Evangelical committed to the Church of England you are liable to be divisive in the C of E, and then the Archbishop will say X is divisive, therefore one wouldn't appoint him as a bishop.

'One trouble is that so many Evangelicals are now hostile to the institution or the establishment, for example, and the Charismatics are not interested. Younger Evangelicals have grown up into a student world of renewal-style worship, very relaxed, no robes at all: that sort of thing. They're at odds with the institution that pays them. There's a younger generation for which Reform is the great new hope. They have their leaders: Tony Higton, David Holloway, Phil Hacking; there's always one major movement in every generation. In mine it was the Eclectic Society, and that was very influential for reform within the structures, but Reform is standing against the structures, and shouting about them.'

Canon Saward continued: 'I've always been prepared to use the word Evangelical of myself, I'm in the Reformation tradition, but if you're a careerist, then no way; it's a millstone. People call you a fundamentalist and all sorts of near libels, and it's a disadvantage. You have to explain the whole time. Yet if you look at world Christianity *en masse*, Anglican Evangelicals are dead centre, at the pivot point, though no one spots it, or says so.

'If you are genuinely an Anglican and an Evangelical – which I am – well, I see myself at the pivot point of Christianity. I can perceive the vital importance of catholicity, that it is a very important element of historical continuity, and I'm prepared to argue for the threefold ministry and the creeds. I quoted the Fathers more than anyone else in the General Synod, I never quoted scripture, or they'd say, "That's what you expect from a Bible-bashing Evangelical. But then you see I'm an Evangelical Anglican. Now Reform want to use "Evangelical" as the noun and "Anglican" as a sort of adjective.'

Michael Saward is an Anglican first and an Evangelical second. The positioning of the noun and adjective says a lot about the divisions on the Evangelical wing, and it is more than a subtle difference. 'I'm an Evangelical first and an Anglican second,' says the Revd Philip Hacking, Vicar of Fulwood, in Sheffield, the chairman of Reform. 'Yet I'm an Angelican of the historical kind, I love the liturgy; but I find I have more fellowship and friendship with Evangelicals of other demoninations. In Reform we would argue that we are good Anglicans and good Evangelicals, but that could change.

'I could not continue to minister in a Church which legally authorised homosexual clergy,' he declares, moving swiftly to what has become a prime concern among Evangelicals. 'Many would find it meant withdrawing from authority. It would mean greater division than we had over the women. A lot of lay people are bewildered, and just can't understand what the Church is doing.'

Withdrawing from authority, or at least threatening to withdraw, is a mark of Reform which bothers Evangelical bishops as well as diocesan authorities. The movement gathered a thousand members in its first three years, 'more lay than clergy,' Phil Hacking says, 'though not much so. It is a largely Evangelical movement, but some Anglo-Catholics have joined who feel Reform offers a better bet than Forward in Faith.'

Evangelicals, like other groups, are divided over the ordination of women to the priesthood. On this issue, those opposed are alongside the Catholic traditionalists, though for different reasons. For them headship is the important question, the biblical imperative that makes women unacceptable in positions of leadership. Some Evangelicals belong to Forward in Faith, and have been in that largely Catholic movement since it was launched immediately after the Synod vote in November 1992. Liberal Evangelicals, like liberal Catholics, are often enthusiastic supporters of women priests.

'Reform started with the issue of headship, after the ordination of women, but now the homosexual issue takes up most of our time, and we see it as probably coming to a head fairly soon,' says Phil Hacking. 'Because we're Bible-based, our view is on biblical grounds. There is a grey area over women, even for me, but not with homosexuals.'

There are, he explains, several kinds of Evangelicals. There are classical ones, and Charismatics, of whom Reform has quite a number, but also liberal Evangelicals, 'though they don't use the word themselves. They went to Evangelical colleges, but it doesn't mean that they are Evangelicals now,' he says. 'Among the Charismatics there are a lot who are not "Toronto", and are very upset about things, and have formed an association. When people say Reform is creating yet another division, it hurts.'

The division is largely over money, for Reform believes in keeping back funds from central bureaucracy and putting them into parishes. Several big Evangelical churches already cap their quota, but Phil Hacking says, 'It isn't withheld, it's diverted. There's one parish gives £1000 a week in quota. One of the things we do is to support a priest in Sheffield. We believe the local Church should have more freedom.'

Reform knows it is not much loved by fellow Evangelicals, especially those in the hierarchy. 'They regard us with some suspicion and a certain amount of alarm. We may be seen as aggressive. But Evangelicalism is a broad concept, and there are those who sympathise with us, though they wish we had started on a different wicket. They are eirenic and don't want the boat rocked: but it's being rocked already. Some just want to get on with the work in their parishes, as I wish I could. Well, we're organised before the homosexual thing comes upon us like a flood, and many will join us over that issue. I hope the bishops will have the courage to stand – but I doubt it.'

An Evangelical Leaders' Conference at the beginning of 1995 was warned by Bishop Michael Baughen of Chester to stop guerrilla warfare and sniping denigrations unless they were to miss their chance again, as they had in every century since the Reformation. 'I beg you,' he said, 'don't let history repeat itself for the fifth time.' The Bishop touched a common chord when he declared that homosexual intercourse was contrary to God's law, but a *Church Times* editorial observed, 'As a method of obtaining unity among Evangelicals, exhortation has its weaknesses. The larger and livelier the movement, the more it will have to struggle with internal disagreements.'

Trevor Stevenson, the executive officer of the Church of England Evangelical Council, is one of the eirenic people mentioned by Phil Hacking, for he organises the council's Assembly, where, he says, the general spirit was very good and understanding in May 1995. 'Reform was there, and the Toronto Blessing people; we maintain close touch with HTB. If you have a common core of belief, and a willingness to differ on other matters, it can hold together.'

The Archbishop of Canterbury, Dr George Carey, at home on the Evangelical wing, was dispelling fears that the bishops might relax their ban on ordaining practising homosexuals. 'The House of Bishops will not be stampeded into changing its stance or

pastoral practice,' he promised. It was an altogether more peace-
able affair. The video that came out of it, *A Highway for our
God*, shows the Revd Graham Cray, the Principal of Ridley Hall,
Cambridge, having an argument with the slightly more radical
Revd Wallace Benn – the kind of discussion Evangelicals love,
about the appropriateness or otherwise of the word 'inerrancy'.
They agree that they are on different sides of the fence, 'but so
close we can hold hands'. Graham Cray says, 'Our disagreements
have been about appropriateness rather than the core, the complete truthfulness of scripture which we both want to affirm.'

Another thing both these gatherings affirmed was the desirability
of church planting, an almost totally Evangelical crusade, reviewed
in a glossy Church of England report called *Breaking New Ground*.
The report arose from a Board of Mission working party, commissioned by the House of Bishops and chaired by the Bishop of
Southwell, the Rt Revd Patrick Harris. It says the average rate
of church plants since 1990 has been one a fortnight. Nearly all
are Evangelical; many are ecumenical; some are across parish
boundaries.

Problems, surely? Only a few, says the report. 'In a few cases,
no more than four that we are aware of, new congregations have
been planted without the approval of the bishop and the local
clergy. It was these cases, and the questions they raised, which
led the House of Bishops to appoint the working party.' Perhaps
the four include the one which arrived uninvited in one town
centre to the fury of the diocesan Bishop and the annoyance of
the vicar, who was himself an Evangelical. Some of the PCC had
defected and returned to the home patch to plant. St Andrew's,
Chorleywood, is an energetic planter, so is Holy Trinity, Brompton.
HTB is one of the big, well-staffed churches which can well afford
to send a curate off with a hundred people to start a new congregation. They crossed the diocesan boundary into the diocese of
Southwark – with permission – to colonise St Mark's, Battersea
Rise, which was dying when the new blood took it over, and now
it thrives. Many of the people who went there were 'yuppies' who

lived on that side of the River Thames and had been travelling over to HTB.

But when a take-over like this happens, a church's tradition can be changed overnight, and congregations which are struggling may well wonder whether they would like it to happen to them. In practice, people who cannot settle for it leave, and the rest are swept into the dance.

Only a minority of plants take over churches which are up against it but still functioning. The Revd George Lings, Vicar of St George's, Deal, and a leader of the church plant movement, collected the figures for the report, which came out in 1994. Of the 177 plants then known to him, 107 rented schools, community centres or other public buildings, fifty used existing churches and church halls, and eight were in private houses. Only five plants were in the country. Sixty per cent were in areas with a strong church presence, which means places with the most privately owned houses.

The question that planting raises is about parish boundaries, for as the Archbishop of Canterbury, a keen supporter of church plants, told a church planting conference at HTB: 'Our understanding of the Church is rooted in episcopal leadership and parochial structure.' The report finds no difficulty in this.

The Bishop of Southwell sums up its conclusion in his introduction. 'Finally, the working party believes that church planting is not an erosion of the parish principle of mission in the Church of England. It is a supplementary strategy which enhances the essential thrust of the parish principle – a commitment to a ministry to all members of a community, individually and collectively, within the overall commitment to establishing and sustaining the Kingdom of God.' There is, he says, 'no room either for aggressive empire building or for last ditch defensiveness'.

One thing non-Evangelicals would like to know is how big Evangelical churches raise huge sums of money, apparently by praying it in, for there is a feeling that 'it wouldn't work for us if we tried it'. Michael Saward says, 'Evangelicals believe in God, and in his power liberating people emotionally and financially. They pray, and he uses his power. Or, of course, a crowd attracts a crowd. As a schoolboy, if you shouted "Fight", half the school would come out to watch, if you called "Debate", no one would bother. There are questions about the potentially manipulative element that can crop up. I hope my style isn't, but I'd know how to do it. It simply means you have to do something closer to the tabloid sort of thing.'

One Evangelical church that knows the secret is Pip'n'Jay, SS Philip and Jacob, in the heart of Bristol, on what is thought to be the oldest worship site in the city. The church has kept the old Saxon form of James – which is Jacob – and is almost certainly the only one in the country with that particular dedication. John Wesley preached from the Jacobean pulpit (circa 1631); the American evangelist, Billy Graham, just stood in it and never said a word, during his Mission England campaign in 1984. All Dr Graham wanted was to have his photograph taken in the pulpit once occupied by Wesley, the vicar, Canon Malcolm Widdecombe, recalls.

Pip'n'Jay pulls in money to give it away. When Malcolm Widdecombe first came on the scene as a young curate in the early sixties, the population of the parish was moving out, the church was left with a small, elderly congregation and enormous maintenance costs, and the diocese was thinking of closing it down and letting it be used as a potato warehouse: 'a sure sign that the church had had its chips,' he says. With a group of young people who wanted to use the dilapidated church hall as a youth club, he began the long process of reversing the situation.

A growing congregation cleaned, cleared, built and painted, while the diocese watched the old potato threat receding, and in 1974, as it celebrated its 800th birthday, Pip'n'Jay was rewarded with the promise of a future. Malcolm Widdecombe was instituted as its vicar. And by December 1993, 'a sort of anniversary', since it was thirty years on from the beginning of their new life, the congregation chalked up its first £1 million for missions.

It has sent out a baker's dozen of missionaries of its own, half of them with wives who share their ministry, and it also gives to

Evangelical missionary societies like Tear Fund. Canon Widde-combe says, 'We expect to reach our second million in the next ten years. We split the money among our own missionaries, seven units for a married couple, four for a single person. How do we do it? You've only got to look at our motto: "Seek First".' It comes from Matthew 6:33: 'But seek ye first the Kingdom of God and his righteousness, and all these things shall be added unto you.' For Pip'n'Jay, it has turned out to be true.

The altar (Evangelicals call it the communion table) is covered for communion services with a cloth which bears the 'Seek first' motif, worked specially for Pip'n'Jay by nuns of the Priory of Our Lady of Peace, at Turvey Abbey, in Bedfordshire. 'We got our motto from the People's Church in Toronto, which discovered in the great depression of the 1930s that it's impossible to outgive God. They're no relation to the Toronto Blessing, they're conserva-tive Evangelicals, and we are, too, but also a bit Charismatic.'

A Toronto Blessing team did pay a visit to Pip'n'Jay, but accord-ing to the account of it in the parish magazine, *Seek First*, the Spirit behaved quite circumspectly on that occasion, and in spite of multi-decibel music, one or two people fell asleep. 'We had the good side of it,' the vicar says. 'There are certain questionable side effects: T-shirts that say "I'm a jerker for Jesus." I agree with one Evangelical who said that's sick. But if people are refreshed by Christ, which is what we have found, it's good.

'As far as the future goes, the homosexual lobby is the next big one for Evangelicals. If they ordain practising homosexuals a number of churches will go UDI. There are a growing number of Christians who give loyalty, not to the institution, but to the church to which they belong.'

His views on women priests, whom he cannot accept, make him feel isolated to some degree. 'We have a strong liberal Evangelical Fellowship in Bristol. I was the only one who voted against women priests, and I resigned. I've found better fellowship with other ministers. We have a weekly prayer meeting for revival in the city.'

Prayer is an important part of the action at Pip'n'Jay. 'Not as many as I would like pray, but with those who do, it's quality praying. Once a month we have either a day of prayer and fasting on a Sunday in church, ending with Evensong, or half-a-night of prayer, from eight till midnight, or all-night prayer from 11 pm to 6 am. We're orthodox, but not tied to the liturgy, in fact we have everything from dancing in the aisle to evening prayer. I, personally, love the old *Book of Common Prayer*, and use it for what we call "the masochists' mass", before breakfast on Ascension Day and saints' days, and if there's no saint's day, we make one up. Not many people come, just a handful, because we're an eclectic congregation, two hundred on the electoral roll, and an average sixteen at *BCP* services on weekdays; but we're not number-conscious at these.'

They do not seem to be number-conscious at all, yet the money rolls in. The parish magazine says simply: 'It is a miracle of God's faithfulness, and proof positive that God's word is true. To him be ALL the glory.'

CHAPTER EIGHT

Where There's Smoke There's Fire

> *What though the mast be now blown overboard,*
> *The cable broke, the holding anchor lost,*
> *And half our sailors swallowed in the flood?*
> *Yet lives our pilot still.*
> *(King Henry VI, Act 5, scene 3)*

THE INCENSE RISES; and the greater the festival, the more it billows out in a sweet-smelling cloud which is bliss to those who love it and anathema to those who do not. The thurifer swings the thurible for all he is worth, ignoring some rather pointed coughing by one or two people with handkerchiefs pressed to their faces. The candles shimmer, the lamps by the statues are lit, and in the chancel the disciplined worship flows on.

There is, however, more than one kind of Catholic Anglican. Evangelicals are not the only ones with divisions. Catholics of a liberal, mild and eirenic nature are often drawn towards Affirming Catholicism, not a party, but now a movement, they would say. Its members are anxious to shed the Catholic reputation for being negative about certain new developments in the Church. They prefer to affirm, and for most of them, if not all, that means affirming women priests. People ask about a Catholic priest, 'Is he an Affirmer?' which actually means, 'Does he accept women celebrating?' If he does, though he may not be a paid-up member of Affirming Catholicism, he is taken to be in sympathy with the movement.

Dr Jeffrey John, Vicar of Holy Trinity, Eltham, and formerly Dean of Divinity at Magdalen College, Oxford, incensed traditionalist brethren at the time of the Affirmers' meeting in York during July 1995 by saying: 'Thousands of loyal Anglican Catholics in the

Church of England have been told that their faith is finished in the C of E. We must help them see that they still belong in the home they have, and that not one jot of our Catholic inheritance has passed away. From now on, Affirming Catholicism *is* the Catholic movement in the Church of England.'

That is where the difference bites. In the letters page of the *Church Times* of 28 July that year, the Succentor of St Paul's Cathedral, the Revd John Lees, replied: 'Jeffrey John should have been at the Bishop of Richborough's consecration to the episcopate [that of the third flying bishop, the Rt Revd Edwin Barnes]. Then he would have seen that Affirming Catholicism is not the Catholic movement in the Anglican Church – merely, at best, part of it; and some of us doubt that, since it patently sacrifices more than "one jot of our Catholic inheritance".'

Premature reports of the death of the traditional Catholic wing in the Church of England have been circulating ever since the vote for women priests in November 1992, some of them from inside the Catholic wing itself. Yet with two of the three highest offices in the Church held by David Hope at York, and Richard Chartres in London – both from a Catholic background, and neither of whom ordains women priests – things might have been thought to be looking up.

The result of the 1995 General Synod elections was not as dire as was feared. Though 155 traditionalist Catholics stood as candidates, the Catholic Group in Synod [which does not include Affirmers] was reduced to less than than half of its previous strength of 170; but the shrinkage was fully expected and might have been worse. 'I was pleasantly surprised,' said Arthur Leggatt, who was then general secretary of the traditionalist Church Union, which was founded in 1859 at the time of the Oxford Movement, 'to promote Catholic faith and order'.

There is a feeling that the 'two integrities' acknowledged in the Church of England cannot hold, and a suspicion that the three flying bishops, the Provincial Episcopal Visitors who were consecrated to support the traditionalists, will not be replaced when they retire. They are all in their sixties. 'I have grave doubts about whether it will hold together. It's very difficult for a Catholic with a strong ecclesiology,' says the Revd John Salter, Vicar of Wantage in Oxfordshire. 'I perceive that it is those bishops who one might have thought were Catholics, those with a Catholic ecclesiology, who can't cope with it at all. They are the ones I'd say are most aggressive. They can't cope and they don't see that it has a future.'

Fr Salter's parish has been in the Catholic tradition since the great Tractarian William John Butler arrived there in 1846 to begin an incumbency which lasted thirty-four years. He became a Canon of Worcester afterwards, and ended his ministry as Dean of Lincoln, but he has gone down in history as 'Butler of Wantage', because the real work of his life was the daily 'faith, prayer and grind' he commended to the battalions of curates he trained over the years, who went out from Wantage like sparks through a cornfield, lighting up the darkest places of misery and want in the cities of Victorian England. Alexander Heriot Mackonochie, the great priest of St Alban's, Holborn, was one of them.

Butler cared about gaslight and drains, about social action undergirded by prayer and worship, which has always been the Tractarian style. He founded the Wantage sisterhood, the religious community of nuns which is there today as the Community of St Mary the Virgin. 'Anyone who knows anything of the history of the Catholic revival in the Church of England cannot suppose that it was opposed to the ministry of women – quite the contrary,' said one of the preachers at the 1994 celebrations of Butler which marked the anniversary of his death. That was Dr Geoffrey Rowell, now Bishop of Basingstoke, speaking not about priesthood, but women's ministry. Wantage has stayed in the Tractarian tradition, the worshipping of God in the beauty of holiness.

Dr David Hope, then Bishop of London, spelt it out when he joined in the Butler celebrations: 'Those early struggles about the wearing of vestments, the use of candles on the holy table, the reservation of the sacrament, were never intended to become struggles simply about the sanctuary and its ornamentation.

'Rather these were the very means, the outward and visible signs and symbols of the inwardness of these holy and awesome mysteries which would lead the worshipper more deeply and fully into the death and resurrection of the Saviour, thereby enabling us truly to live his risen life in every aspect of our lives day by day.'

Fr Salter says he sees Dr Graham Leonard, a former Bishop of London who became a Roman Catholic priest, as the person with the vision for the future. 'We'll see a Pan-Protestant Church, in which the Baptists are strong, and Catholics in union with the Pope will be strong. Catholics in the Church of England will melt away.' This was the prophecy of Dr Leonard: a realignment across the religious board.

John Broadhurst, chairman of Forward in Faith, told the movement's national assembly in September 1995: 'We have accepted that we are a minority in the Church, for whom special, and probably temporary, arrangements have been made. We intend to survive and grow like a faithful remnant, but they intend us to die.'

That 'they' are awaiting the death throes is open to doubt. The Bishop of Richborough painted a brighter picture, saying that all three flying bishops had been talking to the Advisory Board of Ministry about ways of encouraging more orthodox Catholic candidates for ordination. In any case, 'Catholics have always fought. There's a history of it,' says the Revd David Houlding, Vicar of All Hallows', Gospel Oak, in London. He became a new member of the Catholic Group in the General Synod in the last elections. 'We can't moan and complain if we don't take part in the debate.'

The Affirmers, on the other hand, feel that they are Catholics who keep the faith but still move on. 'The point I have reached is an extraordinarily radical point,' says one of the movement's leaders, Canon David Hutt, of Westminster Abbey. 'I think that I recognise the Church of England to be part of a historical European development, and that what the Elizabethan Settlement did for me was to guarantee an essential catholicity without the Church of England becoming Calvinistic. There was a sort of deal done, which did, strangely enough, have overtones of two integrities. And then I of course discovered the Caroline divines, and all of the Oxford Movement, and I felt very secure in this tradition.

'The churches I used to go to were very sound in a sort of 1930s sense. I look back pretty well forty years to St Augustine's, Queens Gate. Here was something redolent of European catholicity, but somehow it was still very Church of England, and I was nourished by that tradition in no uncertain manner. The daily mass; devotions on Saturday evenings; Benediction; and then an hour of silence in a church lit only by sanctuary lamps, the incense rising . . . one could actually hear the angels. It was an extraordinary aesthetic experience, which people like Compton Mackenzie have written about. So I was very much drawn into the Anglo-Catholic culture, but I was a realist, and I thought, well this has got an authentic place in my Church of England. Later on I discovered the great heroes of the docklands and the East End, who were very firmly rooted in that tradition.

'I have to say that eight-and-a-half years at All Saints', Margaret Street, was very spoiling, because the ritual was very disciplined, and it was not a distraction, so the combination of elaborate ceremonial and the music was very uplifting, and I think that good worship does that, and has always done so. It's almost in line with the Old Testament, with Isaiah, and the idea of the holy mountain: being drawn to the numinous in the area of worship. And then of course I used to travel about and find Anglo-Catholic worship being done very badly, in a very slipshod way, and that I found depressing, because some years ago I discovered Quarr Abbey, on the Isle of Wight, of a Benedictine tradition, and there was an extraordinary severity of style, great simplicity, with vestments of the simplest in design, and nothing was unnecessary. I must say my heart leapt at that, and I think I have to say now that lace and frills don't have the compelling power that they used to have.

'I talk about those externals because I think in a way they helped us through a period of transition, when Anglo-Catholicism became, first of all, academically impoverished. The great scholars in that tradition are no more, and it is difficult today to think of great scholars except for Rowan Williams [Bishop of Monmouth];

Richard Holloway, who would rather humbly describe himself not so much as an academic but as a spiritual journalist; and David Jenkins, who would claim to be a Catholic, but would, of course, be written off by most people as a complete maverick and charlatan, and I don't think it would be fair to include David Jenkins in an Anglo-Catholic context.

'It's actually very difficult to recognise the inheritance of that great tradition of scholarship, always part of the Anglo-Catholic faith. And the other thing that does concern me enormously is the loss of a certain ascetic spirituality. I don't want to be too sweeping, but I just want to say that the great heroes of the past, men and religious women, were profoundly men and women of prayer; and I think that this rooted them, it gave them courage, it made them radical, and it helped enormously their work with the poor. The social gospel was actually powered by prayer: action, issued from holiness, if you like.

'I think now, the Anglo-Catholic movement has really run out of steam, and it means there isn't the fast-forward movement, there is a looking back and a slowing down, a retrenchment and a defensiveness, and a loss of joy. And for these reasons, I find myself an Affirming Catholic, very sad to have been struck off some people's Christmas card lists.'

Canon Hutt continued: 'What's happened, I think, is in the Church of England we have become very parochial, in the broad swathe of the Church's adherents, and we're becoming more and more conditioned by culture. It's arguable that we have always been conditioned by culture, but somehow, in the past, the Catholic heroes have always managed to transcend this.

'I think we have never had a great link with the working class, but in the past there was some credibility, and now we have rather lost out. And of course with young people today, this sounds very gloomy but I think it's true, it isn't the Catholic parishes, but the Evangelicals who draw them, and I'm very sad that younger people who aspire to follow Our Lord are sometimes not fed. There's a way in which to be young is to be identified with a peer group which some of the Evangelical parishes have really got on board, and it's very exciting. At Holy Trinity, Brompton there are young professional people who find themselves in the ecstatic tradition. They don't choose to go to a Catholic church in London, they go there.

'It concerns me rather, because numbers are clearly diminishing, and instead of seizing the opportunity to say, "This is perfectly all right, we don't have to be afraid of death, because that somehow brings us very close to the essence of Christianity," there is a sort of pretence that everything is going to be all right, eventually. I don't think it will, in those terms. The Catholic movement as we have known it and loved it has actually got to die.

'Where Affirming Catholicism comes in, it began as a movement of reaction to things like extreme Anglo-Papalism, things like double-speak about sexuality (and that of course is clergy-code for homosexuality); things like authority – much claimed for the authority of the Church, but little shown in evidence for the diocesan bishop.

'Sadly, catholicity is by definition non-evangelising, and I think what's happened is that, as in Roman Catholic parishes and dioceses, the faithful are looked after, the lapsed are sought, the Catholic families are nourished, but there's never been any sense of the need to go out, and this is a very serious challenge for the Church. What we as Affirming Catholics must do is to recognise that this stage of reaction – and I think it was a healthy protest at the time – has now got to be bettered by some very serious theological inquiry. This is the great area of hope and expectancy. We've got to look very, very closely at what we mean by the Church Catholic.

'The hard work Affirmers have now got to do is to get together people and scholars who can safely make a determined claim for catholicity, because the alternative is something not even Evangelicals would want, a bland Pan-Protestant body, where the Church association is of a happy-clappy kind: and there is nothing against that, but it is a threshold stage rather than a fulfilment. All those caught up in the Alpha course, which is admirable, and is commended by bishops, have little to say about the sacramental life of the Church; and this is where people have really got to be able to realign sufficiently to say that the spirit matters, that God matters, that Catholics can, with confidence, test their faith in the face of increasing secularisation of society.'

The Church Union, founded in 1859 to promote Catholic faith and order in the Church of England, grew out of the Oxford Movement, the Catholic revival, and any Affirmers who belonged to it will have left it by now, for it is traditionalist, opposed to the ordination of women to the priesthood, though it is broader-based than most of the other Catholic societies, says Arthur Leggatt, who was its general secretary until early 1996, and is still secretary of its International Bishops' Conference. It was the CU which established Forward in Faith immediately after the General Synod voted in favour of ordaining women priests.

There are about 4000 Church Union members, laity and clergy. 'The vote affected us. We lost people, but not as many as I thought we might, and we were compensated for the losses by new people joining, but not entirely. Many went to the Roman Catholics or the Orthodox; and of course we lost some through our opposition. We did not believe that the General Synod had the authority to alter the nature of the ordained ministry. Quite a large section of the Anglican Communion is still unsure.

'We have got to think that there is a future. As the liberal agenda unfolds it will have a continuing effect on Catholics in the Church of England. As a body we shall become much more marginalised than now, but the Church Union is well-placed to give support as people become more so. Our part will be continuing to defend and promote the Catholic faith, and many of those unable to accept women priests will have to take up the role of defending it through litigation, as they have at St Luke's, Kingston.'

St Luke's, a traditionalist parish in the diocese of Southwark, which opted for alternative episcopal oversight from the Bishop of Fulham, as under the Act of Synod it was entitled to do, went to court to challenge a decision to suspend the living and give it a part-time priest. Because it had passed the resolutions provided under the legislation – that it would accept no woman celebrating or pronouncing absolution in the parish, and no woman as incumbent, priest-in-charge or team vicar there – it did not fit into the pastoral scheme for the area. 'It's lots of things like that,' says Mr Leggatt. 'We support litigation rather than initiating it, and that is why we have established a legal committee. We have contacts in the legal field we can turn to for advice.'

The Church Union is well aware that Evangelicals are better than Catholics at attracting children and young people. Its Children and Young People's Committee is working on this. 'We're always very good at the big events, like the Walsingham Youth Pilgrimage, but it's the steady drip drip drip of water on stone every Sunday,' says the Revd Ronald Crane, Priest-in-Charge of Washwood Heath, in Birmingham, a largely West Indian parish in the care of the flying Bishop of Ebbsfleet, surrounded by Muslims and Irish Roman Catholics. He is giving a lot of thought to the problem against a background of his own successful experiments.

It worries him that Catholic parishes use material provided by the Evangelical Church Pastoral Aid Society and Scripture Union because it is colourful, jolly and well-produced, and also because it is there. 'But the ecclesiology it's based upon fits uneasily with what we teach, and then we wonder why we get into such a mess. The Bishop of Horsham, Lindsay Urwin, is chairing a small group of six or seven to produce our own material, then if that's viable we have to get the finance. As he says, it's having the will. We can produce things as good in quality as the Evangelicals.'

Fr Crane has visions of a source-book magazine for Catholic parishes, available by subscription, with easy-to-prepare lessons, visual aids and music suggestions; a group identity for children up and down the country, with badges and sweat shirts. He plans for the future because he is someone who hopes there still is one. 'I think the Provincial Episcopal Visitors are the hope. They are all splendid individual people.'

For an isolated Catholic priest in the countryside, and in a not particularly sympathetic diocese, things are not so clear-cut. 'You have to accommodate all sorts. For lots of our people, their real home would be in the Free Churches, and we go from them to about half-a-dozen on the Catholic wing, and everything else in between,' says the Revd Douglas Clarke, who has four little churches in rural Hertfordshire. 'You have to steer a central course, but you do get in the teaching. You keep the saints' days, but however much you teach, there are those who would never go. The thing is not to lose heart, but to go on providing, whether people want it or not. The most important thing is to love the people and teach as far as possible. If there are fewer than seven people on a saint's day we go to a parishioner's house. We have a mass round Amy's kitchen table. It's a very lovely, intimate service.

'Everything is much more intimate in the country. You're known by everyone in a much deeper way. If only the Church would concentrate on people instead of money, the money would take care of itself. More and more clergy are being withdrawn from parishes – I descend on a village and then vanish again from their midst – but if you take away the leader, how are you going to build up the Church? Most laity are busy people; it just doesn't work that way.

'But locally ordained people – our former Bishop dismissed it, he said, "What if they move?" Well, if they move they move. If we had a locally ordained person in each place, having a weekly meeting with a fully trained priest, they could look after their own little village but under the guidance of a fully trained person. That's what Catholics ought to be doing.'

There is one little village that draws Catholics together from every part of the country, from Newcastle to Truro, all through the year on parish pilgrimages, but especially on Spring Bank Holiday for the national pilgrimage, when five or six thousand people converge on the Shrine of Our Lady of Walsingham, in Norfolk. Coach after coach rolls down a leafy lane that leads to 'England's Nazareth'. Middle-of-the-road parishes go too, but the ambience is very Catholic, and the blaze of candles in the Shrine Church has to be seen to be believed.

The church contains the Holy House, a model of the one the Lady Richeldis built in 1061 at the behest of the Virgin Mary, who appeared to her at Walsingham and asked for a replica of the home at Nazareth. The shrine was destroyed in 1538 – though in godlier times King Henry VIII used to go there as a pilgrim – but in the palmy Anglo-Catholic 1920s Fr Hope Patten, the Vicar of Walsingham, restored it, and it has flourished ever since, working closely now with the Roman Catholic shrine a mile down the road, which is positively austere by comparison.

The national pilgrimage always attracts a stalwart gaggle of extreme Protestants, Anglicans and others, armed with banners about the blasphemy of the mass, who shout and sing all day opposite The Bull, the pub where the clergy gather. 'Dare to be a Protestant; Dare to stand alone.' They reach a crescendo when the image of Our Lady is carried in procession, but they are part of the scene, not a bad-natured lot on the whole, when you talk to them, and in a way their now familiar faces are an accolade for the really 'Catholic' nature of a splendid day out for the parishes.

Walsingham is one of the things that makes the Archbishop of York, Dr David Hope, believe that Anglo-Catholics in the Church of England are not finished yet. 'I felt at Walsingham there was a very good crowd, not quite as many as usual, but a good crowd of people and a good crowd of priests.

'And I always say to the number of clergy who come to see me that at the end of the day the strength of the Church of England is in the parishes. The Tractarian movement grew out of fervent, committed, dedicated and disciplined parish priests who had a great indomitable zeal, who loved the Psalms, and set before them that transforming vision of God's Kingdom come on earth as it is in heaven, and I still think there's a very considerable place for that. I think there are numbers of priests and parishes where there is evident witness and testimony.

'I wouldn't take so pessimistic a view of the future, because actually I think of some of the things for which our forbears fought, and some of the things they had to endure – I mean I was in the parish of St John Tuebrook, in Liverpool, which was under the Bishop's ban for years and years, with nothing whatever to do with the Bishop, and they got on. They produced ordinands, they produced religious; a lively parish, with people going to church; sacraments faithfully administered. When a bishop from abroad came through, he was got hold of, confirmation candidates from years back were lined up, they got confirmed, and that was it. So I don't see that it's necessarily doomed or there is no future.

'Will there be a realignment? Well, I think it's very difficult to predict, but again I don't think I'm into preserving Anglicanism for the sake of it, because the universal, the Catholic Apostolic Church, is larger than that, and if the Church of England has somehow to die in order to live a different sort of life, that will happen in God's good time; so I wouldn't be over-worried about that.

'I think I've got to be optimistic about the life of the Church, because the Church is the expression of the risen life of Christ, the transforming power of Christ in our society and our world. I think if you believe in God, you've got to be optimistic, really. I've said throughout the women priest business, to the clergy, you know – I'm given today. All right, there is the perspective of tomorrow, I do think about tomorrow, but I'm actually given today. It's today that I actually have to speak words of faith and life and hope to the people I meet. There has to be that kind of commitment, that recognises that God is at work, and as for the rest, I can leave it to him.'

CHAPTER NINE

Great – and Greater

Great buildings and soaring arches are so that Christians may have somewhere to play at heaven. (Canon Michael Perham, in a Barry Memorial Lecture at Southwell Minster)

THERE ARE PLENTY OF ROWS in the Close. Cathedrals are not as peaceful as they look. Everyone knows that now, after the battle of Lincoln, waged between the Dean and the cathedral canons. It stemmed from a loss of £56,000 through the exhibition of the Lincoln Magna Carta in Australia, and Margaret Thatcher's subsequent appointment of a Dean with a confrontational style which had the effect of a spark tossed into a box of fireworks. Lincoln became a happy playground for the tabloids, who were back there in 1995, when Dean Brandon Jackson was tried by a Church court and acquitted of allegations of sexual misconduct with a former woman verger.

There was trouble at Salisbury between the cathedral and the wife of the then Bishop over a plan for a new road through the Close to solve the traffic problems, and further friction when Bishop John Baker produced a highly critical visitation report which appeared to accuse the Dean and Chapter of commercialism; though Bishop Baker, a kind and gentle man, subsequently expressed regret over hurt feelings. St Paul's, in London, is plagued by staff upsets. Peterborough, a cathedral in the traditional style, with Anglo-Catholic leanings, has had its upsets over the appointment of a Dean who has been described as 'wildly Evangelical': the Very Revd Michael Bunker, the former vicar of an Evangelical stronghold at Muswell Hill, in London, which he built up over many years in a manner reminiscent of Archbishop George Carey's achievement at St Nicholas's, Durham, in the 1970s.

Hereford became the centre of a national storm when it tried to sell its Mappa Mundi, and although that episode ended peacefully, it was one of the reasons behind the formation of the Cathedrals Fabric Commission for England. Deans and chapters must now seek approval before they carry out any plan affecting the cathedral, its contents or surroundings, from the Commission in some specific cases, or from a local Fabric Advisory Committee appointed jointly by the Commission and the Dean and Chapter.

According to one cathedral dean, there are other cathedrals as unhappy as Lincoln, 'only it hasn't leaked out'. And yet, cathedrals can be a foretaste of paradise to those who go in search of something outside and beyond the limits they impose upon themselves. Durham, seen from the train, takes your breath away, Peterborough crouches like a great beast, the thrill of the first distant view of Canterbury never fades, and Lincoln: 'Sometimes it seems to float above the city,' said a priest who sees it every day.

'If you've got to have a pile of stones you might as well have it look like this,' says the head verger at Lincoln, John Campbell, who lives within its shadow. 'It all goes on here without any heed of adverse publicity. I think a greater force is looking after it.' Lincoln is known for the chill of its vast and splendid spaces. 'We have improved the heating, but when we have a concert here you can always pick out the locals. They're the one with blankets.'

He has served at Winchester, one of the great Benedictine foundations, Bradford, a parish church cathedral in a diocese founded in 1919; and rose-red Carlisle, small and valiant, possibly the most lovable of all the cathedrals, because it is, as Dean Henry Stapleton says in a guide book, 'a building complete in the beauty of holiness'. Carlisle is nearly 900 years old, built on a site where Christian worship goes back into the mists of time, and it makes the veil between earth and heaven seem thin. John Campbell feels 'almost homesick' when he thinks of it, but now he has Lincoln, and 'You have to have your loyalties where they are.'

Vergers, he says, are in the front line at any cathedral, the first people the visitors see, and whether they are in cathedrals or parish churches, they have a ministry which the Church of England has only recently begun to acknowledge. Mr Campbell has completed a busy stint as general secretary of the 800–strong Guild of Vergers, which has evolved its own training scheme, a four-unit course based on Open University principles, with a diploma at the end of it. 'Vergers are helping themselves to be better-educated to do a job in a changing world, where the demands are different,' he says. They are not just caretakers now.

'If we can turn tourists into pilgrims, that's good. We can't always do it with the hordes we get, but sometimes people write. There was a man from Liverpool, with his wife, who stopped me and asked a lot of awkward questions, and after twenty minutes or so the conversation turned humorous. Three weeks later his wife came to see me again. She said he had come in a depressed state, and the banter had lifted him out of it. I hadn't detected that he was depressed, I just thought perhaps he was out for a bit of a contretemps, though he didn't get it; and she had taken the time and trouble to come and tell me.

'Once I had a gun pulled on me in the vestry, though the woman was not going to use it on me. She had come all the way to Lincoln from Surrey to commit suicide. Over four days I got her back to her husband and connected her with a local priest. We're a sort of magnet for God's problems. These places attract them, which is just as well, or where else would they go?

'If you sit someone down in the nave and walk a quarter-of-a-mile to look for one of the clergy, twenty or thirty minutes will go by, and the person will think he's been rejected. You have to recognise when you need good back-up, and we have a booklet we refer to, with names people can call on with marriage problems, or for deliverance. We look on ourselves as first-aiders, not to see people through to completion, but to be there when they first fall.'

Once he was showing a party of schoolchildren a cadaver, one of those tombs with an effigy of a great man dressed in all his finery, while above him a grinning skeleton presents a contrast difficult to regard with any degree of complacency. 'I told them about princes and paupers, and how they all end up the same, and asked if they could see the moral of this. One child said, "Yes. Don't sleep on the bottom bunk."

'Sometimes the more basic the question you're asked, the more doors it opens. It may be telling them about the doctrine of baptism, because they don't know what the font is. That's the variety of the job, you never know what's coming. It's a pot-pourri of things, which hopefully smells sweet at the end of the day.'

Each of the forty-three cathedrals has its own ethos, but the one most different from the others is Coventry, whose distinctive vocation began for it on 14 November 1940, the night German bombers dropped 500 tons of explosive on the city in the worst single raid of the war on any town in England. Coventry Cathedral was decimated, so badly burned that only the spire and four charred walls were left standing. Basil Spence's new cathedral has risen beside them, a great church, full of light and space, with its patron, St Michael, treading down the devil over the entrance. Yet when you go there it is to the ruins you look, for they are magnetic, and when you stand before the cross made out of two charred roof beams there is a sense of spiritual power which is almost tangible. 'Father Forgive' is carved on stone behind an altar open to the sky from which destruction rained down, and those two words tell Coventry's story.

On Christmas Day 1940, Provost Dick Howard stood in the rubble of his cathedral to broadcast to a nation at war, saying: 'Hard as we may find it, we Christians say, "No revenge." We will try to build a kinder, simpler, more Christ-like world in the days beyond this strife.' And that is the work that has continued, 'both a ministry and a mythology, now half-a-century old,' says Canon Paul Oestreicher, Coventry's Director of International Mission.

He works in a small room under the ruins, built by young Germans out of the wrecked vestries, dark and churchy, in contrast to the new cathedral over the way, and the only spot where you can breathe in the authentic ecclesiastical smells. There is not a whiff of hymn book, hassock or wax in the Basil Spence building, and no dim corners to hide in, but here the old atmosphere lingers.

Paul Oestreicher was once a German-Jewish child, hiding in

cellars and fleeing for his life from the Nazis, and since 1986 he
has lived out Dick Howard's message of reconciliation through
Coventry's Network of the Cross of Nails Ministry. The chromed
cross he wears is one of the originals, made from the fourteenth-
century iron nails from the roof beams, which were found lying
in the ruins after the bombing, and gathered up by a young priest
who worked them into crosses in his garden shed. The first one
went to Stalingrad; today they are all over the world, though the
300 nails ran out, and the newer crosses are chrome all through.
Paul holds his cross as he talks of Dick Howard.

'He was a charmer, very humble, and never very well known,
though the things he was doing were as visionary as the things
George Bell, the then Bishop of Chichester, was doing, and he, of
course, became an international figure. Without Dick Howard this
cathedral would never have spoken to the world, and this cathedral
would never have been built. His personality was big enough to
influence the city councillors when the war was over, and they
agreed that Coventry should be the symbolic city that went out to
create friendship throughout the world, and between them Coventry was made into a place better known abroad than here. It was
the first to have German twin cities: Kiel and Dresden. The next
Provost was Bill Williams, who ran the building like a battleship
– his brother was an admiral – and he carried out the dream of
his predecessor.'

The German President came to the fiftieth anniversary of the
cathedral's destruction; the Queen went to Dresden, where over
40,000 people were killed in the raids, compared with 1000 dead
in Coventry; and Paul Oestreicher spends a lot of time with the
Churches in Germany. But now he has set himself a stiffer task.
'I'm working on reconciliation with Japan, and that is a hard
furrow to plough. Christians are about half of one per cent of the
population, Christian mission has never taken off in Japan, and
there is corporate amnesia about the last war. Christians there
feel embarrassed to be part of an unrepent nation. We have
taken a beautiful sculpture to Hiroshima (kneeling figures
embracing) and there will be a replica of it in the ruins here.

Ironically, Nagasaki, where the other bomb fell, is the most Christian city in Japan, six to seven per cent Christian, and it is the only place of which that is true. We feel our particular mission is to offer forgiveness to the Japanese, whether they accept it or not.'

Cathedrals are 'shop windows of the Church of England', according to the report of the Archbishops' Commission on Cathedrals, which ran to 262 pages when it was published in October 1994. The commission, which was chaired by Lady Howe of Aberavon, was appointed in the summer of 1992 to examine the future of cathedrals, and it offered them 'admiration and respect'; but it also found 'scope for considerable reform and improvement of the way they are governed, staffed and manage their affairs'.

On the whole, the deans and provosts welcomed the idea of a more professional style of management, and more accountability. 'We like the emphasis on the mission of cathedrals as churches for the nation,' says the Provost of Southwark, the Very Revd Colin Slee, who was formerly Sub Dean of St Albans. 'They were realistic about the fact that we need to trade, that's it's not dirty, that we've got to pay our way; and that was really good.

'Then there is the emphasis on liturgy and musical excellence – girls' choirs – and cathedrals as teaching resources, both the buildings and the education centres, which I'm keen about: the one we started at St Albans had three-and-a-half thousand children the first year, and last year over 16,000. It's so important, because it's teaching about the Christian faith by using the building to teach things like mathematics and geology. You can look at something which is nothing to do with religion and come away touched with holiness.'

Southwark's Provost is a human dynamo who appears to have the gift of bilocation. He is an opportunist with a heart for mission, who sets enormous store by worship; a friendly and informal dignitary in the modern style. His appreciation of the Howe Commission's report has its limits. 'We think the recommendations about governance are dreadful, and that they have completely misunderstood the way cathedrals function, and most particularly, parish church cathedrals, with genuine congregational participation.

'We think that the business of the bishop chairing a greater council is a complete nonsense. It contradicts the historic balance between the dean and chapter on the one hand, and the bishop on the other in a diocese. You go back to the Reformation for that, and it was a very wise and shrewd move. Of course most bishops and most deans get on tremendously well, but there are places where there needs to be someone in the diocese who is, as it were, free to stand in opposition to the bishop on occasion; and the dean in chapter is therefore a very helpful and thoroughly Anglican counter-balance: and vice versa, I may say.'

Southwark, an inner-city cathedral, has a reputation for social action and innovation which Colin Slee wants to recover. 'But in fact my first task is to put together the administration and the finance to give us the freedom to do it. That's what is so exciting. A number of things have fallen into place, like five major City businesses saying, "Between us, one of us will second you an administrator, free." They are going to find a member of staff, a young executive who needs stretching, and lend him or her to us. Now that sort of co-operation is fabulously encouraging.'

Didn't the Howe report say that every cathedral should have an administrator? 'It did. And what it failed to address throughout the report was the question of financing its recommendations. I think it fell into the old trap of looking into cathedrals which have considerable resources and therefore assuming that everyone can do it: and the Blackburns and Southwells and Southwarks of this world aren't in that league. There, I think, is a weakness in the present arrangement for the Cathedrals Fabric Commission, which is that English Heritage grants on a mutual basis – we put in some money and they give us a percentage; and the banding is insufficiently weighted in favour of the poor cathedrals. It is weighted in their favour, but not enough. I think that will mean – and this is classic – that the rich get rich and the poor get poorer. So St Paul's, who've got to rebuild their dome, get promised hundreds and thousands of pounds, whereas others, like Blackburn, who need hundreds of thousands, can't get promises because they haven't got hundreds of thousands to put up to match it.'

Southwark must reach out to the homeless, he says, 'and the victims of the so-called care-in-the-community policy. We constantly have mentally disturbed and subnormal people wandering in here for warmth and shelter who have just become derelicts, because they've been thrown out of mental hospitals, and really can't handle life. I want to build a day attendance centre and a counselling service for people with those sorts of needs, and I think we should be addressing racism, which in the inner-city, you rapidly discover, is black on black, and black on brown, and brown on yellow, as well as white on everything else.

'Another side of the coin is that the entire South Bank from Greenwich to Lambeth Palace is just exploding, and I believe the cathedral should be in touch with big businesses of the inner city on very friendly, cordial terms which enable it, somehow, to be a host. We have twenty-seven corporate carol services.

'Being a cathedral church gives one a remarkable platform to talk to judges, members of the Cabinet, MPs, charitable trusts and councillors. So I think there is a ministry to the people who have the lonely jobs at the top of their particular pinnacle.

'Lastly – and here is the great conundrum – if we're going to thrive we must be centres of interest and tourism, and earn our keep. Yet our purpose is to be an oasis of quiet and space and stillness. How do you put those two contradictory demands together? It used to be that everything was so secure, that the past was there, and all would be well. But the new generation of deans and provosts has a different approach: that if we go on like this, we'll be broke in twenty years' time. It makes us rather hard-nosed, in a way, and that is not good. But if you can get a hard-nosed canon doing it for you, then perhaps you can be a scholar and a holy man as well, and that's the great advantage of a chapter. Look for your mix of skills and personalities. If you're all bubbling Scorpios full of energy (yes, I am) then the poor congregation will be worn out. But if you've got someone who's wise and prayerful and someone who's elderly and experienced, someone who's pastoral and loving as well as someone hard-nosed and businesslike, and someone else who's a scholar, then you can put together a team that enables the cathedral to offer a spectrum of ministry.'

A visitor flow wears out floors and adds to the cost of maintenance. Cathedral appeals are reaching astronomical figures, and although about £4 million a year of Government money has been distributed among cathedrals in recent years it is a drop in an ocean of endless and enormous need.

Yet one sentence in the Howe report reaches the heart of the matter: 'We have been struck by the continuing capacity of cathedrals, in a world which is often depicted as secular and materialistic, to stir the hearts and minds of men and women of all types and conditions.' But then, of course, it depends what people are looking for. One day in York Minster, which is great and glorious, like *The Messiah* in stone, the staff were dismayed to see an old lady in tears, clearly in deep distress, and some of them advanced to the rescue. They drew near in time to hear her say to her daughter, 'You promised to take me round Woolworths and Marks and Spencer's, and you've brought me to this dump.'

A cathedral, one might think, is an unmistakable sight, but this is not necessarily so. A mighty building towering over a little town or village or looming up in the inner-city might be one of the greater churches, bigger than some cathedrals, and even more of a headache to those who love and care for it, because they have to manage without any of a cathedral's resources.

The Revd Eric Woods was once a curate at St Mary Redcliffe, in Bristol, so he thought he knew which of the greater churches was the fairest of them all, and Queen Elizabeth I would have agreed with him; but when he had his first sight of Sherborne Abbey, in Dorset, the effect was 'staggering', he says; enough to send the senses reeling. It would be possible to go from one to another of most of the greater churches and be similarly smitten time and again.

Although greater churches look like cathedrals, they are parish churches, each a colossus in its little patch, far too big for the parish, hugely expensive, obliged to earn a living as cathedrals do, with gift shop, coffee bar and visitors' centre, but without a full team of vergers and other staff. Thanks to Tom Flynn, the former administrator at Tewkesbury Abbey, the greater churches have come together to talk about solutions to the particular problems they share. Mr Flynn is the honorary secretary of the Greater Churches Group, which grew out of his experience at Tewkesbury, where he saw the difficulties of trying to provide homely parish worship in a building of gargantuan proportions, though he says the clergy are getting very good at making people feel at home.

He divides the greater churches into two types: the abbey minster models in a real parish setting, and some huge, busy, city-centre churches with a weekday ministry to shops, offices, market traders and visitors, and on Sundays to a congregation which travels in from outside. The ministries of the two types are different, but they have problems in common because they are all untypical parish churches.

Leeds Parish Church; St Martin's, Birmingham; St Mary's, Nottingham; St Mary Redcliffe, Bristol; St Peter Mancroft, Norwich; Croydon Parish Church, and Holy Trinity, Hull, are greater churches in city centres. Monastic models are Beverley Minster, Christchurch Priory, Bath, Hexham, Romsey, Selby, Sherborne and Tewkesbury Abbeys, Wimborne Minster, and Malvern Priory. Those are the members of the group so far, whose clergy and administrators spend time together under one roof every two years to exchange ideas.

Canon Michael Moxon, the chairman of the group, was Vicar of Tewkesbury Abbey before he became a Canon of Windsor. 'Tewkesbury is bigger than about fourteen of the cathedrals,' he says. 'The group is a mutual support ring, to help them bear their burdens, hopes and fears, and it's about the bread-and-butter way of running things as well as the spiritual side: visitors, finance, the need for extra staff, problems of damage, insurance, VAT . . . and there's still the little old lady round the corner who's just lost her husband.' As a former parish priest he hits on the most important thing, for with all their particular problems, the greater churches hold fast to their parishes.

'Incumbent's wide span of attention' was one of the 'problem areas' discussed at the second greater churches conference, in November 1993. In November 1995 the theme was user-friendliness, which began to look even more important when the Dean of Bristol, Dr Wesley Carr, sowed the thought that the chief user of all that space is God.

Nearly 1300 years of history had rolled over the Abbey when Eric Woods became Vicar of Sherborne in 1993, 'It was the cathedral of the West Saxons when the great diocese of Winchester was last split, in fact it was a cathedral until after the Norman Conquest. We consider ourselves Salisbury Cathedral's grandmother,' he says. 'Wulfstan expelled the secular canons in 998, and asked the Benedictines to run it, so the Benedictines were here when the see was transferred, and in fact until 1540 [at the dissolution of the monasteries]. That was when the Abbey was wondrously saved, because the people of Sherborne had always resented losing their cathedral to the monks; they had always thought of it as their church, and the monks were never accepted by the town. People were happy to get rid of them.' Not that they have anything against religious these days. 'Hilfield Priory [home of Anglican Franciscans] is in the deanery, and I regard it as another resource, a source of spiritual enrichment. We draw heavily on Hilfield.

'Sherborne is a very live parish,' the vicar says, 'but there are lots of county obligations, lots of extra-parochial demands. Sherborne School is next door, the vicar is a governor, and the school uses the Abbey as a chapel, because they can't all get in to theirs. Then there's Sherborne girls' school, and the vicar is chaplain there; and Church of England comprehensive and primary schools; and a Roman Catholic school which has a lot of Anglican girls.

'I love the parish itself, but I occasionally feel it's getting second best. I'm a visiting vicar; I've tried hard to make it feel it comes first, and I try to get to our other churches. The town is very proud of the Abbey, and works closely with it, so raising funds for the building is never difficult, and the town council maintains the close. But really the priority is still to be a parish church for the people, though a great church like this is not very user-friendly for many people. We're expected to be a centre of excellence for liturgy, and I can't say to wedding couples as I did in a village, "Come and see what we're about."

'We have a council estate, and there are liturgical and social barriers, which is why I'm glad to have a little church, St Paul's, on the estate. We can't be happy-clappy and informal in the Abbey, the building is so stately, so it's desperately important what we offer in our other churches. I wouldn't want to be vicar just of the Abbey, because a varied community needs a varied diet, which would be impossible in just one church. I've suggested to the Vicar of Tewkesbury that he might bring a team to do a parish audit here, which would be one great church helping another.'

There are choral services every day in the Abbey. 'We have a very charismatic choir master. There are sixteen boys from the town at any one time, and gentlemen, and it's unashamedly all-male, because the day the girls came into the choir, the boys would all leave. There is, however, a move towards an all-girls' choir, and that I would encourage.'

One thing the great monastic abbeys have plenty of is space: vast, uncluttered areas of light and height and silence, which Dean Michael Mayne of Westminster Abbey has said must be used to give people a sense of the transcendent, to help them look beyond the stones. But into huge, holy spaces as well as small ones, controversy breaks through. At Sherborne, it has been over a sixty-foot window by Pugin in various reds, depicting a gallery of twenty-seven prophets and patriarchs who by 1995 were looking in poor shape on account of some faulty firing by Pugin's assistant, so a consistory court was told. In the teeth of opposition from the Victorian Society and the Council for the Care of Churches (CCC), the Revd Eric Woods and his PCC decided to raise £200,000 for a new 'Tree of Life' window by the stained-glass artist John Hayward, which they hope to have in place by 1998.

A long legal wrangle ended in January 1996, when the Court of Arches, the ecclesiastical court of appeal, dismissed an appeal by the Victorian Society and found in favour of the parish – and the Tree of Life. Eric Woods sees the affair as 'the first skirmish in much bigger war'. There is an enormous row going on in the glass world, he says, and the battle is really between the stained glass artists and the conservationists. 'Art historians take the view that there isn't a stained-glass artist alive fit to be commissioned for a large window.' The debate continues.

CHAPTER TEN

Corridors of Power

> *While proper place must be given to a process in which the abuse of power can be recognised and resisted, the Church should encourage those with gifts to use them in service to the whole body . . . (The Turnbull report)*

'IT'S A VILLAGE, REALLY; people live here. There's a sort of village square, and a lovely garden out the back.' Bishop Frank Sargeant has been waiting hospitably on the front steps, smiling a welcome as he must often do while visitors make the journey from the gatehouse, past the huge fig tree by the Library wall, beside the magnolia in the courtyard, and up to the big front door of Lambeth Palace. The Palace lies across Lambeth Bridge, on the south side of the River Thames: the London home and workplace of the Archbishop of Canterbury and his personal staff.

At Lambeth the corridors of power are thickly carpeted, and lined with portraits of former archbishops, but the life-style of the residents is not as grand as might be imagined. Who could settle to 'Match of the Day' in the vastness of the state drawing room? Dr Carey and his wife, Eileen, have an apartment upstairs, and the Sargeants are some of their neighbours.

Bishop Sargeant, the former Bishop of Stockport, is the Head of Staff at Lambeth, a friendly man from Lincolnshire, who was Archdeacon of Bradford and director of in-service training in that diocese before his consecration. 'I grew up at Boston, where my father was a Reader at Boston Stump, and he ran the Sunday School. He took me to football on Saturdays and church on Sundays. I used to go the Mothers' Union with Mum, so it's rather gratifying that I ended up as Central Mothers' Union Chaplain.' That was not a job to be taken lightly, for the Mothers' Union, restructured and influential, has gone far beyond its patchwork quilt image.

Bishop Sargeant's study, next to the Archbishop's, at the top of the main staircase, looks over the garden recreated by Rosaline Runcie and now maintained by Mrs Carey's Garden Committee. About forty people work at Lambeth, including part-timers, domestic staff, the gateman, the chauffeur, the gardeners; and as no one in this small and busy world is after anyone else's job, they are said to co-exist in fair harmony. Bishop Sargeant says, 'A lovely thing was that on the Archbishop's sixtieth birthday there was a lunch for everybody, everybody was invited, and the junior member made the presentation to the Archbishop. That was at the invitation of Mrs Carey; so in a way it's like an extended family for those sort of occasions.

'When Princess Margaret came, the Archbishop and Mrs Carey invited everybody to meet her in the state drawing room, so that was really very thoughtful. And we keep birthdays, and we have farewell parties when people leave. Our juniors tend to go to good jobs from here, they're well-trained, and the standard of work here is very high, because if it wasn't, we would go under, because of the pressures. Lambeth is full of capable people. I was only saying to the Archbishop the other day, "Do we just recruit nice people, or do they become nice people working here?" We'd like to think it was perhaps a bit of both. There are no rivalries, that is not a difficulty, because most people have their clearly defined roles, but our difficulty is keeping each other informed when we do have a definite part to play – letting everyone know what the total scene is; that is sometimes difficult.

'It is very, very busy. I always thought I worked hard as an archdeacon and a suffragan bishop, but it wasn't as hard as I do now. Well, it's constant, but everyone is working for the benefit of the Archbishop, and that is very unifying, and people are very supportive and helpful.'

Is there a special Lambeth view of Dr Carey which the rest of the Church does not see, a journey round the Archbishop which only those closest to him can make? 'Yes, that's right, there is,' the Bishop says, 'and if you wanted my own personal reaction, I don't think that I've ever met anybody who's as gentle yet as tough as he is. It's a very strange, unique combination.

'He won't present anything unless it's been through his own word processor, he works incredibly hard. The other thing is his overseas visits; they can be very tiring, and he's in constant demand, he could spend all his time abroad, in the Anglican Communion. And of course we see the whole world visiting here, when ambassadors call, and also people who are going to be ambassadors in other countries: they come and visit before they go to take up their posts. The Archbishop stays in embassies whenever he can.'

Diplomatic connections at Lambeth are maintained by the Secretary for Ecumenical Affairs, Dr Richard Marsh, and the Secretary for Anglican Communion Affairs, the Revd Andrew Deuchar, in the post which used to held by Terry Waite. The Public Affairs Secretary, Dr Andrew Purkis, keeps a watch on the home front, liaises with Parliament, and maintains contact with the bishops in the House of Lords.

Every day can bring surprises. 'But by and large,' says Bishop Sargeant, 'I know I'm going to read the post, oh heck, I read all the post that comes in. I've had about a hundred-and-fifty letters today, but it can shoot up to five hundred, and – I'm told this, but it hasn't happened in my time – if there's a particular issue raging in the Church, it can reach enormous proportions. I think Lambeth Palace is a fairly easy address to remember, and people don't actually see that a lot of the concerns are synodical concerns, and often have to be referred to different people in Synod.

'But I know fairly well what's going to come my way. If there are vacancies on the staff I'm responsible for making appointments, or recommending appointments to the Archbishop. I'm responsible for staff assessments, which we do once a year, and I provide the staff work for the Archbishop in connection with General Synod, and especially the House of Bishops, and the Standing Committee and Policy Sub-Committee [the Church's inner cabinet].

'I'm responsible to the Archbishop and the House of Bishops

for planning the Bishops' Meeting, which is different from the House of Bishops. It's when all one-hundred-and-fifty or so get together. I negotiate with individual bishops, both diocesans and suffragans, over any particular diocesan matter which comes to the attention of the Archbishop, or needs to be brought to his attention.'

The range and variety of his duties puts him squarely in the Pooh-Bah class. 'I'm the link man for the Faculty Office and the special marriage licences. Most of those are routine, but anything that's out of the ordinary is referred to here. I'm also responsible for maintaining the Clergy Caution List, the Lambeth List, for discipline, so I will be in touch with diocesan registrars over those sorts of matters; and I'm constantly in touch with Dr Frank Robson, the Provincial Registrar, Brian Hanson [Joint Registrar and Legal Adviser to the General Synod] and Ingrid Slaughter [Assistant Legal Adviser], who are all incredibly helpful to me.'

Lambeth has its own honours system, which works in the same way as the secular honours list: people write in with suggestions, and in doing so, provide yet another job for the Head of Staff. 'I process the submissions to the Archbishop for the Lambeth degrees, and those come from all over the world, because he has powers to give degrees to people as long as they pay allegiance to the Queen, which of course takes out America. Rather a shame? Yes, well, the Americans think so. Then I'm the point of contact with the Archbishop of York if he wants to be in touch with the Archbishop and the Archbishop's not here, and with the Bishop of London, and especially the Bishop of Dover, who looks after the diocese of Canterbury generally. I'm the point of contact for the Secretary-General of General Synod, the Secretary of the Church Commissioners, the Archbishops' Appointments Secretary, the Prime Minister's Appointments Secretary, St George's, Windsor, and Lambeth Palace Library, which is run as a separate organisation, but we have to keep in touch.

'I'm chairman of what we call the Principals' Meetings, that's the senior secretaries and the domestic chaplain, Colin Fletcher. We meet once a week, and once a month there's a works meeting, to review what work is being done in the Palace and what needs to be done. I sometimes represent the Archbishop at institutions and memorial services, and sometimes attend meetings to hold his interest and watch it for him... in fact I'm sort of generally available to the Archbishop. And that's just about me, I think.'

The long anguish of anxiety for Terry Waite, and, at last, his release from captivity, was before Bishop Sargeant's time at Lambeth. 'The really moving thing is to worship in the Crypt Chapel, which was a place of vigil for him during his imprisonment. I always think, what an appropriate place to make intercessions. Things looked so dark and bleak at one time, when there was no news of him; and then, lo and behold, he returned alive – so I always think that intercessions have a lot of chance of taking hold in the Crypt Chapel.

'We have two lovely sisters on the staff here, from the Community of the Holy Name, and I'm just negotiating with the Reverend Mother for them to stay for five years. They may have to change the personnel, but we shall have the benefit of the sisters. Sister Renate is chapel warden, and she shows people round the Palace; and Sister Beryl is an Aids counsellor, because we think it's very important that the Archbishop is represented in that field. They help us maintain our spiritual round of worship. We have a service, Monday to Friday, at twenty-to-eight, and matins followed by eucharist three days, and then the sisters say their office at five o'clock every day, at which I join them whenever I can, and I find this is the real bonus, for having been a sort of peripatetic suffragan bishop, on the road all the time, to be able to go to church in the morning and the evening is sheer bonus.

'The thing we try to remember all the time is that this is home for the Archbishop and Mrs Carey. We try to protect their privacy when they are at home, and to maintain courtesy by letting them know when people are in the Palace. One of the problems – there's no problem about people asking if they can come round the Palace, because we have guided tours all the time – but it is difficult if the Archbishop wants to get from A to B, and he finds people in the corridor all wanting to say hello to him. That's why Archbishop

Ramsey had these doors put in, as you can see. That's the door to the Archbishop's room, and then that goes out of another door into the domestic chaplain's room, and I think at one time you could get all the way along the downstairs of the Palace without actually going into the corridor. Michael Ramsey was the one who thought that was important.'

The sense of history at Lambeth can be overwhelming. 'The upper chapel is where the Archbishop holds the congregations for his degrees and it's where Cranmer wrote his Prayer Book. There's a room called Cranmer's room. And once,' says Bishop Sargeant, 'I was thinking particularly about saints and martyrs, because we had just got back from Tunisia, where we had seen, in first-century ceramics, an anchor sign on the graves – because an anchor is an early Christian symbol of hope. It's made out of a chi-rho: a cross and a capital P (the Greek capital for R was a P) and it makes the first letters of the Greek "Christos". I thought I ought to be able to find a chi-rho in Lambeth Palace Chapel. I looked all over and found one, in a side window, but then came back to where I'd been standing before, and discovered I'd been standing on one just over the spot where Matthew Parker's bones are buried [Archbishop of Canterbury 1559–76]. In Cromwell's time his body was exhumed and thrown on a rubbish heap, and his bones were then rescued and buried in the upper chapel.

'It's said that it was Archbishop Laud who planted that big fig tree by the Library. He planted it out here, actually, but it was moved, and now it's taking over; and the figs were very good this year, I can tell you.'

The other corridors of power are almost opposite, on the north side of the river, in Church House, Westminster, a stone's throw from the Houses of Parliament (which are referred to as 'across the road'), and in the shadow of Westminster Abbey. These corridors are likely to be shorter in future than they have been in the past, because of changes which are bound to happen in the wake of the Archbishops' Commission on the Organisation of the Church of England, chaired by the Bishop of Durham, the Rt

Revd Michael Turnbull: perhaps not all the changes which were suggested, but some of them.

Drastic slimming-down operations were recommended in the Turnbull report, *Working As One Body*. They were designed to cut through the central bureaucracy, the 'cat's cradle' of overlapping boards and committees, leaving a small National Council led by the two Archbishops to relate to the General Synod and do the things which will still need to be done at the centre.

As the report acknowledges, 'Most of the work of the Church of England is carried out in the dioceses and the parishes', which happens also to be exactly the opinion of the parishes and dioceses. But perhaps it is easy to forget, when you are out there, getting on with it, that 'they', the people in the Church's civil service at Church House, have human faces and Christian names, and parishes to which they catch their trains home in the evenings.

When they leave the centre they play the good layperson's part at local level. Brian Hanson, the Church's chief lawyer, lives in Sussex, and is a member of Chichester Diocesan Synod. Philip Mawer, the Secretary-General, has served on his PCC in Hertfordshire, and before he moved there he was lay chairman of the deanery synod in Reading. Most of his colleagues, he says, are involved in the same sorts of ways. They are all parishioners. So, of course, are the lay members of the General Synod. But a lot of other parishioners out in the dioceses often say that the Synod members are not really representative of 'ordinary' church-goers, the people in the pews' who are mentioned from time to time in Synod debates.

If there is truth in that, it may be due to the curious system of making deanery synod members the sole electors of the General Synod's House of Laity. Not many parishioners want to be on a deanery synod, and practically every parish has the same difficulty when the annual parochial meetings come round. The deanery synod representatives have to be whoever can be persuaded to turn out to the occasional deanery synod meetings.

Philip Mawer considers the question of the supposedly unrepresentative nature of the lay members in General Synod: 'I think it's

easy to make that criticism, because they are not elected on
universal franchise. The House of Clergy is elected by all clergy
and the House of Laity isn't [elected by all lay people]. And I have
to say I have reservations about whether people who get on to
deanery synods and become the electors for the House of Laity
are always appointed to the deanery synod with, at the back of
the minds of those putting them on, the fact that they are electors.
In others words, my experience of getting on to a deanery synod
is that it's a case of "Who can we find to do the job?" and not
"Who do we think would be a worthy representative of us in terms
of casting their vote in a synodical election?"

'But having said that, the Synod is remarkably representative, if
you look at its record. The classic example is the women priest
legislation, where the vote in General Synod almost exactly
matched the voting in the deanery and diocesan synods. It was
one-third to two-thirds in all levels of synodical government. So
that suggests that it's representative. And it's representative in
other ways, too, in that, for example the last Synod had roughly
a third of all its members below forty, a third between forty and
sixty, and a third over sixty; and half the House of Laity were
women. That kind of profile doesn't seem madly out of place when
you look at the people who are in the pews.

'Not that I wouldn't wish for more young people to be represented in the Synod; I would. But if you think about the average
congregation, the breakdown I've given you is not unrepresentative. So I think Synod has proved itself to be broadly representative. Another thing to remember is that no democratic institution
is without criticism in this respect. The Westminster Parliament
itself is criticised for being unrepresentative. We have a Government which is elected on the votes of less than half the electors
in the country.'

Jim White, a Somerset hill farmer who sits in General Synod for
the diocese of Bath and Wells, has long cherished a scheme
for widening the Synod electorate to include everyone on the
church electoral rolls. Philip Mawer says: 'This is one of the issues
before Lord Bridge's Review of Synodical Government Group, and

there are enthusiasts, of whom Jim White is one, pressing for a move towards universal suffrage in the sense that, for example, every member of the electoral roll should have a vote in laity elections. I think the issue there is one of practicalities rather than principle. First, electoral rolls are not always as up-to-date as they might be. Second, you would be widening the franchise to embrace a lot of people who are only occasional attenders at church, and third, there would be a problem of communicating with them, and there is a difficulty already of electors not really knowing the candidates for whom they're voting. In synodical elections we don't have the advantage that you have in a parliamentary election, of widespread media attention during the election campaign; and although electors receive election addresses from candidates, as things stand now many of them won't know the candidates individually. So you would have that problem magnified.

'And then there's a cost consideration. It would be much more expensive. You'd have a lot more votes to count, you'd have the business of distributing many more ballot papers, the collection of those ballot papers, the supervision of the process, in terms of ensuring that, well, that the PCC secretary isn't filling in all fifty. It's a lot more complex if you widen the franchise. It may be that Bridge Group finds a way of making the franchise more representative than it is now without going the full hog.'

But in all the chances and changes, is there a future for the General Synod at all? 'I think it's not difficult to detect the future there, in the sense that there will always need to be a Synod,' says the Secretary-General. 'Synod is not an end in itself. What it is is an attempt to embody a set of practical arrangements on the theological principle that all parts of the body of Christ are represented in the governance of the Church: bishops, clergy and laity; and the Church will always need a body which is its council, that is, its chief council with a small "c", the council in which issues of concern to the Church are debated, policies are decided, and the Church's rules are laid down. So in that sense, it's not difficult to see that there will always be a Synod. How the Synod's organisation is made up, how big the Synod is, what its precise make-up consists of, what precisely its sub-structure in terms of boards and councils is, that is all in the melting pot. It is at the moment difficult to see precisely the way that things will unfold, but I would guess that the move in the parishes, the pressure from the parishes and dioceses to have a more streamlined structure, more focused, at the national level in the Church: that pressure will have to be answered. Whether Turnbull has got in all its recommendations the right answers is a thing the Church is debating, but I can't see the present arrangements remaining unchanged; and I think if they did remain unchanged, there would be, over time, a considerable swelling up of frustration that an opportunity for reform which lay before the Church had not been grasped.'

Whatever happens, the key to the future will have to be more sacrificial giving by Church members. Philip Mawer believes that message is getting across. 'I think that it is. The recent evidence is that giving to the Church has increased well ahead of inflation, and that people have been willing to put their hands in their pockets.

'Alongside that, of course, goes a much greater willingness to question, and that was reflected in some of the pressure that led to the Turnbull Commission. Why do we do things as we do things now? Why are we paying for this? What I think is one of the greatest challenges we face as a Church in this area is to realise, not only that we've got to give more, and give sacrificially, but that we have to give in charity. I mean we have to give, recognising that we don't exist as independent parishes, that we exist as part of the one body of Christ, and that we have an obligation to help those who are less well placed than we may be.

'One of the things the Reform movement is bringing to the fore is the question about what are the limits of giving? Are there limits? Should we be attaching tags to our giving, only giving to those causes or those people that we think are expressing "the right views"? The Church as a whole has got to realise that it lives in mutual interdependence; and that doesn't mean that you shouldn't question what the money is being spent on; it isn't an excuse for sloppiness in the administration of the Church, but none of that is justified. We are under an obligation to use the gifts and resources that God has given us as carefully and as professionally and as effectively as we can. But at the end of the day we are also under an obligation to remain in communion with one another, and part of that is being prepared to support each other materially as well as in other ways when the need is there.

'The other aspect of this is, what is the role of the Church at the national level? As the Commissioners are less and less able to support the parishes, and the parishes assume a greater responsibility for their own funding, then the question being posed by parishes is, "Why do we have to pay for these people at the national level? What are they doing?" I strongly believe that although one of the cutting edges of the Church is at the parish level, particularly in contemporary society, with a mass media and a much more mobile society, there is a task of mission that is as much an issue for the national level of the Church as it is for the local – that, for example, many people outside the Church draw their impression of it, not from what they encounter at the local parish, but what they read about the Church and what it's doing in the columns of the national newspapers.

'So I don't see the parishes and the national level of the Church as being in opposition to one another. I actually see them as engaged in a task which is or should be mutually supportive, and that our primary task is to enable the parishes and dioceses to be more effective in their witness and worship. The parishes in turn have to recognise that there are some things that have to be done at the national level, and indeed which can most effectively be done at that level, and most efficiently, too, and most cheaply.

'You've only got to think, for example, of the work of the Faith and Order dialogue in the area of Christian unity, or the work of social responsibility, the witness that is involved there to the nation as a whole, briefing bishops, and all the rest of it, to see the way in which that work must be done at Church House, or at least, at the national level. It doesn't make sense to replicate it in forty-four dioceses.'

The Turnbull report, *Working As One Body*, carries the same message: 'The Church works most effectively as one body when things are done at the right level. The Church of England does not have and does not need an omnicompetent centre. There are, however, functions which can only be, and have to be, carried out by the Church as a whole rather than in the parishes and dioceses.'

CHAPTER ELEVEN

Ancient and Modern

Only the grace of God can make up what is lacking in the faltering words of men. (Preface to the Alternative Service Book 1980)

'LITURGISTS DO IT RITE', said the Bishop of Salisbury's T-shirt. The Bishop, the Rt Revd David Stancliffe, chairman of the Church of England's Liturgical Commission, wore the T-shirt at a gathering of liturgists in Dublin, according to *News of Liturgy*, whose editor, Bishop Colin Buchanan, feigned shock, and wrote, 'I do not recall Ronald Jasper, for instance, thus clad.' David Stancliffe can carry it off; Dean Jasper, of York, a previous chairman of the Liturgical Commission, would probably not have thought of trying. Colin Buchanan's story, lightly told, could be an illustration of liturgy on the move.

After years of liturgical upsets, the war between defenders of the 1662 *Book of Common Prayer* and the advocates of modern language is not over, but meeting points have been found, and anyway, the Prayer Book is still *the* book of the Church by law established. The *Alternative Service Book 1980 (ASB)* was never more than its title claims, an alternative, though the clergy have often been accused of pushing it to the exclusion of the Prayer Book, and with some justice. Now the *ASB* itself is due for revision by the year 2000, and some things that have been missed will come back again, like real ale.

There will be a mixture of old and new texts within one service, so that the language of the Prayer Book is seen to be valued. The Sundays after Trinity will return, to replace the Sundays after Pentecost, which never sounded very Anglican: a deliberate move to affirm the Trinity in times of comparative religion and the growing presence of other faiths. Canon Michael Perham, of Norwich Cathedral, a member of the Liturgical Commission, told the last General Synod: '... we have warmed to the rediscovery (and that is hardly too strong a word) of the doctrine of the Trinity in relation to Christian belief, worship and prayer. So here is a case where, having looked at a whole series of conflicting practice, we have opted for a well-tried part of our own tradition.'

Canon Perham is the chairman of Praxis, 'an initiative in Anglican pastoral liturgy', which acts as an extra arm for its three sponsors: the Liturgical Commission, the scholarly Alcuin Club, and the Grove Group for renewal in worship, which represents the Evangelicals. Praxis specialises in liturgical education and Canon Perham says: 'We try to make liturgy something people talk about across the traditions. One thing that was extraordinarily successful was when I chaired a day on the future of the Prayer Book tradition. It was the occasion at which there was the beginning of the ceremonial burial of all sorts of rivalries and public posturing, and since then we've seen the end of a lot of hostilities and suspicion. I was invited to address the annual meeting of the Prayer Book Society, at which I received a warm welcome, and that would have been unheard of a few years ago.' He told the Prayer Book buffs, '... the new and the old can be brought together like a kind of seamless robe, providing there is real sensitivity and real care and no shoddiness'.

Inclusive language – which may involve saying 'human beings' instead of 'man', and being careful not to call God 'him' – poses a dilemma for the Liturgical Commission, which says in a report called *Language and the Worship of the Church*: 'Power is moving to those who hear language in a particular way – to groups which feel themselves "excluded" in one way or another by the liturgical language we have inherited.' If these groups hear things differently from most people, perhaps they should just keep quiet? The commission, clearly tempted by this line of thought, says politely that on the other hand, the perceptions of the minority may reflect an important new insight. New texts must be written with sensitivity to gender, race and age. But the Church of England is unlikely to go overboard on this issue, and its use of inclusive language is being well monitored.

The newer liturgies contain material that any parish can fit to its own requirements. This was the point of *Lent, Holy Week and Easter: Services and Prayers*, and *The Promise of His Glory*, which covers the period from All Saints' to Candlemas. The resources they offer are meant to be adapted to local circumstances. 'There will be those who want the Prayer Book and nothing else,' says Canon Perham. 'Others are happy to live in a world of old and new together, but would be glad to see the old given a little more respect.

'We were in danger of undervaluing our heritage – but heritage has to grow and develop.' So the revised *ASB* will be like that: old and new together. 'But you have to be careful what you do,' the Canon says, 'or people think you are putting bits of the Prayer Book into the *ASB* in order to use the Prayer Book less. It's a matter of building up trust.'

'Michael Perham is enlightened,' says the chairman of the 16,000-strong Prayer Book Society, Anthony Kilmister. 'We have been pleased to talk with each other. Neither side will convince the other wholly, but at least we can be more civil, understand each other better, and make whatever turns up in the year 2000 less ghastly.' He thinks the Prayer Book Society has support from many more than its members. 'A lot of people are not joiners, but there are huge numbers out there with a gut feeling. I don't believe there are many words in the Prayer Book people can't understand. A few words might have changed their meaning, but it's the job of the clergy to explain, and if they are too lazy, it's a case of the clergy falling down on their jobs. If you go to the black Pentecostal churches, they use the King James version of the Bible, and they can go on with unwritten prayers for seven or eight minutes without pausing, in Cranmerian English, and they are in the inner cities, some of the most under-privileged people in society.

'Our supporters range from dukes to dustmen, quite literally. There is nothing elitist about the Prayer Book. Those we used to call the working class and those at the top of the tree have been the most vocal, and it's the trendy middle classes wanting to change things. A lot of people voted with their feet and joined the ranks of the lapsed, because the liturgies of the sixties, seventies and eighties actually switched people off. They just stopped coming to church. They haven't gone to Rome, or they'd find it a good deal worse. The present Liturgical Commission is at least trying harder, in fact they are bending over backwards to be as reasonable as possible, but some are mad keen on inclusive language, and that makes for doctrinal changes.'

One change which still makes some people uncomfortable is the passing of the peace in the middle of the eucharist. When the priest says 'Let us offer one another the sign of peace' the response can be a few quick handshakes with the people nearest, a rush round the church with hugs and greetings all over the place, or something in between. The Revd Tom Thorp, at Whitchurch, in Buckinghamshire – where they actually moved from modern-language Rite A to the 'thees' and 'thous' of the Prayer Book-style Rite B – is someone who goes easy on the peace. 'I say, "The peace of the Lord be always with you," and then I wait. Some don't pass it on, some do – but they don't get long. It works quite well.'

Anthony Kilmister says the peace is an absurdity. 'It's so contrived and unreal, getting up at that point and shaking each other vigorously by the hand. It's disturbing and irritating. Why not greet people on the way in or out?' What it signifies is the people of God being together and sharing one bread, but a layman wrote in a Derby Cathedral newsletter: 'Are we to believe that in the dark period of Christian worship between Cranmer and the Alternative Service Book people had no regard for each other, or that those Christians from other persuasions who do not offer one another the sign of peace may, somehow, not fully understand that they, too, "share one bread"? ... I often reflect that God needed to visit Samuel at night in the Temple because he knew that if he came during a service he would not have got a word in edgeways.'

That may be why God often seems to speak through music, which sometimes lifts the soul, and usually stops people talking;

yet music starts more arguments in churches than most things, especially since the new songs and choruses began to displace the familiar hymns. The change is more marked in Evangelical and Charismatic churches, but it filters through to most places, even if it only means 'Shine, Jesus, shine' instead of 'O Jesus, I have promised' when the Scouts and Brownies come. There is always the cathedral sound, the real glory, though even in closes and cloisters, nothing stands still. A growing number of cathedrals now have girls' choirs, following the move pioneered by Salisbury, on the grounds that girls should share in the first-class musical education the boys have always had in choir schools. Their voices are not the same, but some people think they would be, if the girls had the same training.

Girls' choirs sing their share of services, but separately. Not many directors of music in England would expect a mixture of boys and girls to work, though Charles King, the chief executive of the Royal School of Church Music (RSCM), thinks it a possibility, for he heard the mixture at the only cathedral where it happens – St Mary's Cathedral in Edinburgh – and liked it. Resistance to girls' choirs is a generation problem, he says, 'a purist approach as opposed to the practical. It's like the whole question of sex discrimination in jobs. Ninety years ago women didn't have the vote, and in fifty years' time, if by then to use girls has become the norm, future generations of organists will say, "Why not earlier?" But I defy any musician to say that a girls' choir is better. It's a different sound.'

It can be argued that the tribal differences between young boys and girls is as much of a bar to mixing them as the difference in their voices. 'At that age you get one group taking over, and it's usually the girls,' says the Revd Guy Pope, vice-chairman of the RSCM in London. This certainly has been the experience of some churches with voluntary choirs. When the girls come in the boys go out. But Charles King says, 'It depends on the attitudes of clergy and parents.' And a few more years of maturity may swing the balance, for he has talked to directors of music about the problem of keeping the boys, and their answer is, 'Get the girls'.

Going about the country, he has been struck by how many choristers are brothers and sisters or sons and daughters of other choir members, which may be why he finds that there are some areas where church music is 'absolutely thriving'. In other places it is not, but although lots of churches are struggling, more are doing well, he says. 'It is a question of whether they are adapting to the changing needs of the parish.'

Music goes with liturgy, and church buildings go with both. These are the three ingredients of worship and evangelism which were identified when the Archbishops' Commission on Church Music published its report, *In Tune With Heaven*, in 1992; and now the Liturgical Commission, the Royal School of Church Music, and the Council for the Care of Churches are working together to help the parishes achieve excellence. If there is a distinctive Church of England spirituality – and people seem to find it difficult to define – the same three ingredients will be in that, too.

It used to be possible to think of C of E spirituality being lived out in the religious communities on behalf of everyone outside, and to some extent it still is, but perhaps not for ever. 'The single-sex community committed to poverty, chastity and obedience for life doesn't seem to have any appeal for young people, as far as I can see,' says the Revd Malcolm Johnson. He is Master of the Royal Foundation of St Katharine, which is near Limehouse Station on the Docklands Light Railway: a small oasis in London's East End. A big, leafy garden surrounds the quiet house, but the tower blocks in the background are reminders of an urgent theology of everyday living which no one tries to exclude.

Malcolm Johnson is a General Synod member who topped the clergy poll in London in the last two Synod elections. He moved to St Katharine's in 1993, after eighteen years as Vicar of St Botolph's, Aldgate, in the City, which is famous for its work among the homeless, centred on its Crypt. Queen Matilda, who founded St Katharine's as a hospital in about 1147, would have approved of St Botolph's.

Her charity survived the Reformation, because of royal patronage, and was laicised for many years, until monks from the Community of the Resurrection, Mirfield, took over in about 1965, with Sisters of the Church from Ham Common. Men and women have worked there together from the beginning. Now St Katharine's is laicised again. Malcolm Johnson had four sisters from the Community of St John the Divine, Birmingham, and three Franciscan brothers, but they have gone back to their communities now, and he sees the need for changes on the religious scene. 'The number of novices is going down tremendously. Mirfield is losing out, and all the men's orders. Even the friars are finding it difficult. The ordinary old-style religious community does seem to me to be finished, and needs to be reborn somehow, and I really don't know how that will happen,' he says. 'How you give rebirth to the monastic religious ideal is a very difficult question, but I suspect that men and women would like to live in community for a shorter time than for life.

'I remember once, when I was young, asking a religious order, "Could I live with you for a couple of years?" – because I thought it would benefit me in my spiritual life if I were to be part of the community for a short time – and they said no, they thought it was too disruptive to their order. But I think the way forward is to have more communities where it is possible to have two or three years, and that may be a part of what I'm hoping for St Katharine's. We are going to try to have a lay community where there is a commitment to each other. I think communities will spring up where there is a need to do a task, or where people have a need to live together, under God, and with some sort of rule. The elements here are worship, service, hospitality, and always have been since 1147.'

Is there a distinctive kind of Anglican spirituality? He thinks about this, and says 'It's so difficult to know, isn't it? The Office seems to be coming back, thanks to *Celebrating Common Prayer* which we use here. [This is the Daily Office from the Anglican Franciscans at Hilfield Priory, in Dorset, welcomed by many clergy as a liturgical shot in the arm.] Matins and evensong in the ASB, I suppose, are used in most places, but *Celebrating Common Prayer* has enlivened the Office, and made it attractive. It uses many more canticles and other readings, and saves you from getting stale.

'We do a very brisk trade in spiritual direction here. I think half the people who come to me are clergy, many them are on their own, of course, and they find that their spirituality collapses unless the laity come and say the Office with them. There's a woman priest in a tiny village in the Chelmsford diocese who has three or four people each weekday, she invites them to come, and that has really held her steady. It also means that the church can offer the Office each day, and everybody gains.

'I find clergy are hesitant, and say "Nobody will come." And I say. "Well, have you asked them?" You see they haven't asked. But if you say, "I, as a priest, need some help in saying my prayers" – it is a very powerful thing to say, but they've only got to ask, and I think they will find that people will come.

'If we're talking about Anglican spirituality I think it's obviously based on the eucharist. Anglicans have Holy Communion on the brain, they are always on about the mass, or the eucharist, but there is in fact more to Anglican spirituality than the mass, though no one is a stronger supporter of the mass than I am. It has held me steady, like a rock when I've been bereft. But the Office, also, is a very important part of spirituality, as are one's own private prayers, and meditation, and confession . . . all the usual sorts of things.'

What, exactly, is spiritual direction? 'I don't like the term spiritual direction. The spiritual suggests something only concerned with prayer; direction suggests that I tell people what to do. Spiritual direction is really helping people to orientate themselves to God and what he wants for them: the whole of their lives. So I will talk about money with them; how they spend their money, how much they give away, would be very much part of their spiritual direction, as would holidays, retreats, meditation, contemplation, intercession, mass, rule of life, and all those things. Some people actually want a rule of life; others don't. I used to have a rule of life until about ten years ago, I was fairly strict with myself, and then decided I'd had enough, because I spent most of my time wondering if I was keeping the rules, so I threw it away; and I've felt very liberated ever since, not looking over my shoulder all the time. But some people are greatly helped by a rule of life, like the scaffolding to a building.

'I think that's how one sees spiritual direction, and I see people as often as they want, every three months, or if they're going through a difficult patch, maybe more. It's different from counselling; it overlaps, I think. Sacramental confession may come into it. Recognition of one's sinfulness is part of the spiritual life. What you do about it, whether sin matters, how much it matters, what strategy you have in place for coping with it, will come into spiritual direction. Some do make a formal sacramental confession kneeling, while I'm sitting beside them, representing the Lord, and I find an equal number will prefer to talk round all their short-comings and their failures and their upsets, and then, at the end, for me to give them absolution.

'And anointing. I'm delighted that the new service book we discussed in Synod will have a service of anointing. I use anointing a fair amount for strengthening people who have definite tasks to do, or definite crises to deal with.

'In the HIV and AIDS field, which I've been involved with for ten years, one tries to say to the person, "You do not have to be at death's door to be anointed, and you don't have to be anointed only once." That is a big shock to most people. They think it has to be just before you die. So we will have laying on of hands and anointing, and many churches are now having this on one Sunday a month; St Marylebone's do, of course; and that is a very moving service to go to. But it's a question of people actually knowing that, and that this sacramental ministry can be part of your spiritual life, particularly when you have a difficult task to face.

'The HIV field has taught me so much, it really has turned my life upside down: actually seeing people knowing about their mortality and facing their death much earlier than expected. It's rather like the First World War, and the Second World War, I suppose. They had to be ready for death.'

Spiritual direction is really what people ought to be up to in the parishes, Malcolm Johnson says. 'It's one of the jobs of the clergy, isn't it? Do people talk about God with their priest? When I go and see people in hospital – not among the HIV patients; that is immediate, and I don't have any worry at all; we are talking about God, life, death, immediately – but ordinary illnesses: we seem to talk about everything under the sun except that, so I sometimes launch the unpopular question and say, "What is this doing for your faith?", or "Are you finding your faith any help in this?"; and it throws everybody. But it was done to me when I was terribly ill once, by one of the sisters who was here, and I said, "Well, honestly, it's not doing a great deal." Then we had a wonderful talk about pain, and what that meant in the context of the spiritual life.

'You can talk about faith. I find it always does work if you are direct, and you can smile, and help someone to talk, because they haven't got anyone else to talk about it with, and as a priest, that is really why you're there. You're not a social worker, or a doctor, or a nurse, or a friend, you actually are a priest, and as I get older I'm not so worried about saying that. But now I always ring the hospital to see if someone wants me to go and see them. I don't go and visit someone cold. I give them an opportunity to say, "I'm not very well today", so they do actually know I'm coming, and it almost creates an agenda. And I don't go if there are lots of other people there. I usually inquire, and say, "I don't want to interrupt your family." The other side of that is, "I actually want to see you on your own"; and sometimes people do say, "Not today, thank you." '

The Revd David Scott, the poet-priest, left his beautiful, isolated parish of Torpenhow in Cumbria, where there are no sounds but birdsong, and the churchyard looks out into Scotland, to engage more closely in the Church's search for spirituality. He is Warden of the School of Spirituality in the diocese of Winchester, where he also has a parish in the city. 'Most dioceses have someone designated to look after the spirituality, and I'm one of those,' he says. 'In our diocese there's just me, attached to the parish, and I'm a catalyst. I'm beginning to discover that there is a great need for things like spiritual direction, quiet days, and individual counselling. People have been very busy, and there's something missing at the centre. The Church of England has been more used to prayers and meditation, but now people ring up and ask for help. I think there has been a shift from confession to spiritual direction: an hour-long chat about your soul instead of a ten-minute confession. It's a lot more labour. Directors of spirituality in the dioceses meet every year, now, to talk with each other.'

The Revd Dr Jeffrey John, Vicar of Holy Trinity, Eltham, and formerly Dean of Divinity at Magdalen College, Oxford, found a huge hunger for spirituality when he returned to parish life. In *What is Affirming Catholicism?*, which he wrote as one of a series of booklets he has edited for Affirming Catholicism, he quotes Archbishop George Carey, who called the religious communities 'the best-kept secret in Anglicanism'. Dr John names what he says is Anglicanism's second-best-kept secret: the sacrament of reconciliation – confession – which he says badly needs resurrection from the dead. 'It is no use Catholic priests arguing in Synod for the right to say "I absolve you" [which they did, for many hours] if no one sees the use of confessing their sins anyway. Somehow we have to get over the Dave Allen-type caricature of confession which has made it ridiculous in popular perception.'

'There are millions of people burdened with guilt who need nothing so much as to hear the words "I absolve you",' he writes. 'To be able to say with authority, "You are forgiven, you are wanted, you are loved; now go and *live*" – that is an enormously healing thing, a gift which no one but the Church can give.'

CHAPTER TWELVE

The Longest Part

> The Church with psalms must shout,
> No doore can keep them out:
> But above all, the heart
> Must bear the longest part.
> (Antiphon, George Herbert)

WHATEVER THE FUTURE HOLDS, and assuming it will not be the Second Coming, which the parish magazine of St Mary's, Luton had heard might take place in the year 2040, it is as well to remember that no tree grows to the skies. Unlike the Church of Rome, the Church of England, when winds of change assail it, goes on much as before, or at least that is how it seems in the parishes. Things might even get better.

Dr David Jenkins told *Third Way* magazine that he thought disestablishment was inevitable, but who would want to take a bet on that? Only an established Church can exist for those outside it as much as for those within, and Archbishop George Carey said something to that effect in his presidential address to the new General Synod: 'We are anchored in the life of wider society in special ways. Let us make our established status work in support of the kind of outward-looking Christian commitment to God's world which should typify all Anglican churches. Such a sense of affirmation of Anglicanism will, I believe, lead not to arrogance or complacency, but to a sense of gratitude for something God-given, to be cherished and valued along with the distinctive gifts of other Christian denominations.'

The Bishop of Portsmouth, the Right Revd Kenneth Stevenson, began his episcopate in December 1995 with the same desire 'to articulate a much greater sense of self-confidence in the Church about its role in relation to the rest of society. Many of the problems we face are exactly the same as face the rest of society: the position of women, for example; and money. We can go forward ecumenically with less apologising for ourselves. I don't want an arrogant Church, but we can be a self-confident Church.'

In his enthronement sermon Dr Stevenson highlighted the Church of England's talent for handling diversity: 'something precious in its blood to present to the world'. Public taunts would come the Church's way, he said, 'because as an established Church we are in the front of the firing line'. He thinks the Church has let itself believe some of those 'expert' comments, but his own conviction is that: 'In the Anglican animal there are resources for facing a very exciting future.'

In spite of the turmoil of recent years, the bitterness of battles fought and lost, and the loneliness of holding fast to what others have let go, the Archdeacon of York, the Ven. George Austin, now looks to the future with something approaching optimism. He believes that a kind of evangelical catholicism already in evidence will grow in strength and fill parish churches with a new vitality and spirituality that can draw people in and keep them.

But a great deal depends on the future of the ordained ministry. The clergy need an adequate system for job-security as the freehold is gradually eroded; firm grounds for feeling confident about their leadership role in partnership with the laity. The number of those offering for ordination will not go on falling forever, but if it is to rise the Church will have to do more than talk about its commitment to the ordained ministry.

The Archbishop of Canterbury has promised that the Church will support the clergy. 'As we emerge from our concern with the increasing financial demands upon the Church nationally and upon each diocese,' he told the Synod, 'I hope we shall be able to send out a strong signal to those in the ordained ministry that they are cherished, and that we have no intention to cut back on our numbers. Colleges and courses need this assurance.' So vocations are to be encouraged, and not stifled by considerations of cost.

Theological colleges and courses suffered a long period of

anxiety and uncertainty while an assessment group weighed up
their prospects and made recommendations which led to the closure of Chichester, Salisbury and Wells, and, subsequently, Lincoln;
and now new methods of theological training are beginning to be
considered.

The Archbishop of York, Dr David Hope, is someone who can
see scope for improvement: 'Well, it's got into a mess, really. The
trouble has been a principle of adding on. We've put in a bit of
this and a bit of that, and now we've got introduction to sociology,
introduction to psychology – all the little bits and pieces, when
what we really need to do, I think, is to take a close look at what
we're actually providing.

'We do need a much more serious and in-depth grounding in
the scriptures. In my day, in the GOE [General Ordination Examin-
ation] you had gobbet papers on the New Testament, on the Old
Testament, on the actual text: you had to study it, and it didn't
matter which text in that sense. There were gobbets on the *Book
of Common Prayer*. Well, nobody knows anything about the
Book of Common Prayer these days. You had the rubric from
the Marriage Service, and you had to write a commentary on it:
that sort of thing; or from the Catechism.

'I get people from – [naming a prominent Evangelical church]
going on and telling me about what the *Book of Common Prayer*
is, and how we should keep to it, and I say, "It's all right going on
about the Word, but what about the Sacrament?" They begin to
look slightly blank at that point, and I say, "Well, what is a sacrament?" And they've no idea.

'I say, "Right", and reach down the *BCP*: the Catechism. "What
is a sacrament? An outward and visible" – I can remember it still
– "An outward and visible sign of an inward and spiritual grace."
And what is the sacrament of Baptism, what is the outward and
visible sign? Water. And what is the inward and spiritual grace?
The regeneration, you know, whereby we are dead to sin and live
in righteousness. And what about the law of the Lord's Supper?
The outward and visible sign: bread and wine. The inward and
spiritual grace is the Lord's body and blood verily received

nd taken. Would ordination candidates be able to answer those questions? No, they wouldn't; but that's what is meant by grafting t in, so that it all becomes a part of you. It's all of that; we've almost lost it, I think, because in the life of the Church people are not being taught these things.

'I would like to see a much more radical approach to theological training. I think there's a good deal to be said for going back almost to those earlier models, whereby there was a small group of people – we could have them around the country or around dioceses – around one particular person. I remember when I was at Orford as vicar, I could have had three or four, and I reckon I could have provided for them a course of training while they lived in the parish. I could have given them experience of hospitals, prisons, schools, all the rest of it, so that you actually taught them.

'And you could have put them out for a series of seminars or lectures, as well as being involved in the life of the parish, being earthed, rooted; coming to church at seven in the morning and being for half-an-hour at the mass, then coming back in the evening and getting into the whole parish thing: so that the church becomes a sort of theological college. I would also then make sure that they went away for at least a fifteen-day silent retreat; and if they can't do that, well, they shouldn't be ordained.

'I think we've got to take a much more radical approach, instead of jiggering about with which college are we going to close? It's so negative, and everybody feels that the ship is sinking – which it is, actually, if we're not careful.

'I think,' says Dr Hope, 'we need to pull that up by the scruff of the neck, and say, we're going to start again. We're going to do a new thing.'

The prospects sound intriguing. No one can say with any certainty how the Church will look in the twenty-first century. Within a decade the crunch may come with women bishops in English dioceses. Perhaps the C of E will lose its comprehensiveness and cease to exist in its present form; perhaps there will be realignment, a drawing together of traditionalists, and the rest uniting

with the Free Churches. There are many clergy and laity who can
only say, 'I'm staying – as far as I can tell at the moment.'

As far as can be told, most committed Anglicans in England
would stay on board till the band struck up 'Nearer my God to
Thee', and that for reasons not theological, or even logical. George
Herbert's lines to the Church of his birth can still wake an echo:

> *I joy, deare Mother, when I view*
> *Thy perfect lineaments and hue,*
> *Both sweet and bright*

To quote a lifelong parishioner now in her twenties, 'The Church
of England is like your family, isn't it? Some of them may be batty
– quite a lot of them are, actually. But it's still your family.'

ndex